Planting New Churches

Jack Redford

Broadman Press
Nashville, Tennessee

The illustrations used in this book are factual, but certain specifics—names and locations of those involved—have been changed in order to protect privacy and confidentiality.

Plans S-76-A, S-118, and M-152-C in Appendices F, G, and H are from *Plans and Planning First Unit Buildings* by T. Lee Anderton, 1976, The Sunday School Board of the Southern Baptist Convention, Nashville, Tennessee.

Dewey Decimal Classification: 254
Subject headings: CHURCH WORK / / CHURCH EXTENSION / / MISSION
CHURCHES
Library of Congress Catalog Card Number: 78-055694
Printed in the United States of America

Preface

This book is a compilation of the shared experiences of many persons engaged in the church planting business in all fifty states and in more than a dozen foreign countries.

I am indebted to the staff of the Church Extension Department of the Home Mission Board, past and present, in the persons of Quentin Lockwood, John H. Allen, Lyndon Collings, William H. Slagle, Nelson Tilton, and David Benham. Many of the ideas, thoughts, phrases, and concepts have been born from a mutual sharing among us.

I am further indebted to many church planting missionaries who have worked with us across the years, particularly Thomas E. Sykes, Otha Winningham, J. Eldon Jones, and Talmadge Amberson. I am indebted to James H. Currin who taught me the value of fellowship Bible classes, which are basic to church planting.

A great host of pastors, missionaries, and denominational staff persons who have shared in our church planting seminars during the past decade have shared insights in study groups, discussions, and papers. Among this group are sixteen missionaries who serve as church planters in Mexico, Central America, and the Caribbean.

I am grateful for the tutelage and long-suffering leadership of E. Harmon Moore, A. B. Cash, and M. Wendell Belew, who attempted to lead me in two decades of church planting activity.

God used missions professor, R. Cal Guy, to provide me basic missionary motivation and inspiration to make a commitment to a lifetime of planting churches as the cutting edge of all missionary endeavor.

If this book communicates at all, primary credit goes to Dan Martin, news editor of the Home Mission Board, for his tireless hours of work in editing and rewriting so that the desired message will be effectively communicated in this book

JACK REDFORD
Atlanta, Georgia

Contents

SECTION I

The Foundations of Church Planting

The Biblical Foundations

• The Holy Spirit is basic to all that is done in church planting.
• The Bible is foundational to church planting.
• We must maintain the redemptive note in all that we do in church planting.
• People are basic to church planting.

The Emotional Foundations

• Love must permeate all church planting activities.
• Creating a suitable climate is essential in doing effective church planting.
• Flexibility is crucial in church planting.
• We must build bridges to people in effective church planting.

The Practical Foundations

• Church planting is primarily the task of a local church.
• There must be committed human leaders for effective church planting.
• Priorities must be defined for effective church planting.
• Participation planning on all levels is essential for effective church planting.

1. The Biblical Foundations

- ## The Holy Spirit Is Basic to All That Is Done in Church Planting

It was hot in Centerville as Jim Larson walked along. He had been going door to door all day. Now it was at the end of the long, hard, frustrating day. He was tired and, besides, his feet hurt. He had received little response and even less interest in establishing a church in Centerville. Doors had been slammed in his face. He had heard the phrase "We're not interested" time and again.

Now, as he walked down the street, another dog barked at him. It was almost the last straw, but there was one more home on the street to visit.

He walked up to the modest home. "Old people must live here," he thought wearily as he walked by the flowers and plants in the yard and on the old-fashioned porch.

He knocked and Fred Bearden came to the door, politely inquiring what the young man wanted.

"We are considering starting a church here," Jim began, trailing off as he saw the elderly man's expression.

Tears began to roll down Fred's cheeks as he reached for Jim's hand.

"We've been praying someone would come," Fred said. "For years Alma and I have been praying that a Bible-believing evangelical church would come to Centerville. We knew God would send someone. . . ."

The Holy Spirit is the catalyst—the energizer—in church planting; he is as basic to establishing new churches as he is to all that the church is and does. Without him, nothing would happen—no desire, no prayers, no answer.

It is as he acts and interacts that churches are planted. Chemically, the catalyst is the agent which sets other ingredients into motion, energizing, activating, and changing them as he, the Holy Spirit remains unchanged.

It was the Holy Spirit who brought about the desire and prayer of the Fred Beardens in Centerville. It was the Holy Spirit who brought about the long, tiring, and frustrating work of Jim Larson. It also was God's Spirit who brought the Beardens and Jim Larson together. Through his action and interaction, he brought about the planting of Centerville Church, a Bible-believing, evangelical church in an area of need.

Church planting—placing churches in communities where there is an ineffective or inadequate gospel witness—is a spiritual operation. It is not just procedure, mechanics, or practicality, though it can be all those things. Church planting demands the presence, power, and direction of the Holy Spirit if churches are to begin, grow, and flourish.

God promises his followers that we "shall receive power when the Holy Spirit has come upon you . . ." (Acts 1:8, RSV), and that promise is as true and necessary in church planting as it is in any other area of Christian life.

The Holy Spirit has been called the energizer, empowerer, guide, comforter, and more; each of his functions are necessary to church planting because church planting is one of the hardest tasks any human ever attempted. There are multiple obstacles, roadblocks, detours, delays, and land mines. Problems demand solutions. People are resistant, lethargic, uninterested. Suspicion and misunderstanding abound. Church planting is not a task to be undertaken alone; it is a task to be undertaken only after one has sought the direction of the Holy Spirit.

He creates desire in the hearts of people for churches. He opens doors and leads the way. If we are to be successful in planting churches, we must seek him as we begin and continue to seek his leadership along the way.

As he led Jim Larson to the Fred Bearden home, he often leads workers to key people in a community.

Ted Summers had been warned not to visit the Don Nelson home. "He's mean and he hates preachers," people around Newcastle told the young minister. "He's thrown people out of his house—bodily." But Summers went ahead with his visit. He had been in Newcastle

*a month and had begun worship services in the American Legion
hall. The numbers were sparse, and Summers had begun to visit
door to door every day.*

He called on the Nelson home. Nelson had been involved in an
automobile accident and was in the hospital, but he found Mrs.
Nelson at home. He ministered to her, and then presented the gospel
message. There, in the living room, Mrs. Nelson accepted Jesus Christ
as her Savior.

Then Summers followed up and called on Nelson in the Newcastle
hospital. As he visited, he quietly presented the claims of Christ
to the man whom everybody in the community called "mean." Nelson accepted Christ, as did Alf Norgen, who was his roommate in
the two-bed ward.

"Nobody ever witnessed to me before," Nelson told Summers.

The Holy Spirit opens doors so that churches may begin; he leads
at every juncture where leaders are walking hand in hand with
him.

Later in this book, the nine steps to church planting are outlined.
The nine steps are procedure and methods for church planting
which have been carefully tested and evaluated. However, the Holy
Spirit may leap over several of the steps as a new church is started.
Such a jump generally is temporary, and normally he leads us to
plan carefully. He will bless our planning, and if he chooses to jump
any step in the process, he will reveal it to workers who are walking
closely with him.

The Holy Spirit is a basic to all that is done in church planting.

• The Bible Is Foundational to Church Planting

*Pastor George Howard preached that Sunday morning on 2
Corinthians 5:14–21, emphasizing the church and its members as
ministers of God's reconciliation to the world. He urged his small
band of people in Westerly to look around them to determine how
they could be ambassadors for Christ.*

*Lilly Sloan came forward during the invitation. She was a faithful
Christian who regularly attended the church, driving fifteen miles
from her home to attend services. She whispered to Howard that
God had impressed her to begin a witness in the town of Cheyenne,
where she lived.*

With Pastor Howard's help, Lilly began a Bible fellowship in her home each Thursday night. The pastor drove over to conduct the studies, based on Paul's letter to the Romans.

Lilly and the pastor visited her friends. Gradually the study grew to fifteen families, including preschoolers, children, young people, and adults. In eighteen months, thirty-one baptisms were recorded as adults and children made professions of faith in Jesus Christ.

The fellowship, which began in an effort to minister God's reconciling love to the people of the small community, grew and was established into a mission. It then became a full-fledged church, all because Lilly Sloan had a desire to minister God's reconciling love to the small community where she lived.

The Bible is basic to church planting, containing the purpose, the pattern of establishing new churches. Moreover, it is the basic tool for church planting.

The story is as simple as 1–2–3 or A-B-C. Man sinned and separated himself from God. The whole dismal story of man's fall into sin and out of grace is faithfully recorded in God's Word, the Bible.

The Bible shows that God's purpose for all mankind is that man should be made whole through reconciliation with God. To effect that reconciliation, God sent his Son, Jesus Christ, into the world where he lived, died, and rose again, giving mankind a chance to be reunited with God.

The apostle Paul tells us in 2 Corinthians that God reconciled us unto himself not counting the trespasses against us because Christ died and rose again for us. Paul also tells us that this "message of reconciliation" has been entrusted to God's people to spread around the world. The church is God's people on mission to the world.

God's people, the church, have a mission of reconciliation. That is the basic of the Bible. The essence of God's Word demands a person-centered witness and requires that the church reflect God's concern for all people.

Through God's Word, we see the ministry of Jesus that he founded his church with a motley group of people, people in which the established religious leaders of the day were not interested. Jesus challenged and confronted many of the values and religious practices of the day. He never purchased real estate or built buildings; he sparked a movement with no highly structured organizational plan. He succeeded because he was willing to risk.

The Bible gives us the pattern for church planting. A careful study of the book of Acts will reveal the greatest story of church planting in the world. It is not a coincidence that the book also is called the Acts of the Holy Spirit. The thrust of church extension in the New Testament came from the Holy Spirit as he filled the lives of the disciples.

Philip was responsive to the Holy Spirit as he left the great revival in the city of Samaria and went out into the desert. He must have been confused, but he followed the leadership of God. Peter was responsive as he went into Joppa. We must—like Philip and Peter—be responsive to the leading of the Holy Spirit as we begin new churches.

The early church met from house to house, in synagogues, on the riverbank, and by the seashore. It was not inhibited by time, space, or buildings. The emphasis was on people as the disciples went out two by two. They did not go out to seek a choice site; instead they went out to witness about the miraculous life and death of Jesus Christ.

As the Bible *contains* the basic pattern for church planting, it also *is* the tool for church planting. In Cheyenne the people gathered to study the Word of God. They came for nurture, for growth, and for development. The infant church evolves from the first believer, to a group studying the Bible, to a Bible school studying the Word on an age-graded basis, to a full-blown congregation which finally resolves itself into recognizing the church that has been born of the Word and the Spirit.

• We Must Maintain a Redemptive Note in All That We Do in Church Planting

Two pastors, Wylie Fredricks and Jim King, were ministers at sister churches in the sprawling suburbs of a large city. The churches, of similar size and composition, were within ten miles of each other. Both were surrounded by literally thousands of lost and unchurched persons.

Fredricks and King, who had been friends in seminary, came to be pastors of the churches about the same time. Both, realizing they must build bridges to their communities, were very much oriented toward ministry. (Bridge building will be discussed in chapter 2.)

Fredricks, at Sisterville Church, began a day-care center, a program for the elderly, and literacy classes for the people who lived in his community. The program, along with recreation ministries and work with poverty-level people, soon reached 700 persons a week.

King, at Calvary Church, also began work in day-care ministries. He also established work with the deaf, alcoholics, poverty-level people, senior citizens, young people, illiterates, and prisoners. Soon, he was working with some 800 people a week.

King led Calvary to explosive growth. Every Sunday morning people were saved. Each week many people were baptized. The church, which had been averaging 100 persons in attendance, zoomed to more than 1,000.

Fredricks operated the same sort of outreach programs yet remained at 100 in attendance. The ministry program overbalanced the church budget. The hard pressed members rebelled. They asked Fredricks to leave.

Calvary grew because the ministries reached into the community, building bridges. The ministries were the springboard to witness, and witness to professions of faith. The ministries were part of the church, expanding into evangelism and outreach.

Sisterville failed because Fredricks forgot why he was building bridges. He would not use the ministries for evangelistic purposes. "We would be manipulating people if we witnessed to them after we got them in for the programs," he said. Nothing, therefore, was said about Christ or redemption at Sisterville church.

One grew and one failed because one maintained a redemptive note, and the other forgot why it was out on the bridge.

Effective church planting cannot be done apart from evangelism. There cannot be an effective church without evangelism. Reaching the lost and discipling the saved are the twin aims of the church. Evangelism and ministry go hand in hand.

In a new congregation, the major portion of the membership must come from unchurched people. To be effective in church planting, the worker must be effective in evangelism. To be effective, he must believe in winning the lost; he must believe it is necessary for people to become new creatures in Christ Jesus, or he will not effectively plant a new church.

A good church planter must be a person who practices habitual personal evangelism. He must be alert to every opportunity to make an effective witness for Christ. He must train his people in one-on-one evangelism. He must teach the Bible with an evangelistic thrust; he must preach evangelistic sermons and give invitations for people to make a personal commitment to Jesus Christ.

Workers engaged in church planting must do regular, frequent, systematic, evangelistic visitation or else the church will never get its roots down into the community; it can never be truly said to be "planted" in that community.

Churches which are growing are those in which the message of evangelism is kept before the church, with pastor and people sharing their testimony and faith in Jesus Christ at every opportunity. Most churches which are dying are those in which evangelism is neglected or forgotten.

If we get a group of women together for a knitting class and never mention Jesus to them, we might as well have taught knitting in college for credit. If we get a group of children together for tutoring or recreation and never breathe a word about Jesus Christ, we will not accomplish what we have set out to do.

We have set out to build Christ's church, and to do so, we must tell people who we are and what we are doing. People do not become Christians by osmosis. It just doesn't work that way; we have to speak up. And we cannot do church planting without being evangelistic.

• People Are Basic in Church Planting

John Roark was an ineffective mission pastor. He had been working on his church field in Northland for some time, but there were no results. He had not baptized a single person—adult, young person, or child—in more than two years. Attendance dwindled from sixty when he arrived to about thirty.

Denominational leaders ventured to find out why the little church in Northland was not successful. All of the elements were right; there were unchurched people all around, and the area was growing because of a new lumber mill.

Roark was a good student and spent every morning studying and preparing to preach.

He made visits but not too effectively.

The leaders listened to him preach one Sunday morning. It was a good sermon, and would have received an "A" in any seminary in the country.

John Roark gave the clue to his own lack of success when he told one of the men who had come to visit, "I love to preach, but I can't stand people."

People are basic to church planting. They are both the primary resources and the target of concern. People are the reason we begin churches. People are the resources of church planting; from them leadership and funds arise as the needs evolve.

People also are the targets of the new church planting projects. Churches are planted to minister to the needs of people. Churches are not ends in themselves, but are planted to glorify God and serve the needs of the community.

People and people's needs must dominate the thinking of church planters. People—not real estate, not finances, not programs, not buildings. People.

2. The Emotional Foundations

• Love Must Permeate All Church Planting Activity

Cal Guy, missions professor at Southwestern Baptist Theological Seminary, tells a story about taking his family out to eat. They arrived at the restaurant and were greeted—after a while—by a bored, lackadaisical waitress. Reluctantly, it seemed, she took their order for steaks.

As the Guys waited, they noticed that all the restaurant personnel—waiters, waitresses, cooks, busboys, cashiers—wore large, orange buttons emblazoned with the words, "WE CARE."

The waitress finally brought the steaks to the table and disappeared without a word. Guy's sixteen-year-old son wanted catsup for his steak and french fries. Guy tried to flag down the waitress. She didn't pay him any attention. She came by the table, and Guy asked for catsup. She ignored him. He tried to get her attention a third time, but again she went right on by without responding.

After a wait, he finally got her to stop. She brought the catsup. Apparently the "WE CARE" buttons didn't mean a thing.

People are hungry for love—not corrupted, banal, carnal love but real love that says "WE CARE." People crave to see demonstrated love—love that shows "WE CARE." People want someone to love them—love that both says and shows "WE CARE."

In the thirteenth chapter of 1 Corinthians, the apostle Paul tells Christians what love really is. He says we must be motivated by unselfish, self-giving love—loving the unlovely and the uncaring, showing them 'WE CARE."

Paul tells us that love is patient and kind and good, that it rejoices in truth. He says it is long-suffering and hoping. He says it is neither arrogant nor jealous but instead is unselfish. He says only those things done in love will last.

The church of Jesus Christ was truly born to care. Despite that, many people see the church—particularly a new church—as one which says "WE CARE" but, like the waitress, doesn't show much evidence of real love. The new church, to become a part of the community, must evidence real love for the community by demonstrating that it cares.

The new congregation must not appear to be a parasite on the community, seeking things from the community for its own interest. It must not seek special favors. Churches sometimes can be justly accused of a "dip-and-drop" mentality as they seek to boost numbers. Then they become cymbal concerts in which people and preacher just rattle around.

If a church is to gain community acceptance, it must do so through demonstrated love. The church must bring a new dimension of ministry to meet needs that exist. Workers must identify community needs and build a program to meet those needs. The planter's response to a community's hurts shows love far more than mere words.

Love opens doors and makes a way in the hard places of the world. Demonstrated love for people through ministry gains community acceptance and helps spark church growth.

Love is the key; but it must be real love, and it must be demonstrated. It must say, "WE CARE."

• Creating a Suitable Climate Is Essential in Church Planting

Ron Anthony has been serving a church in Vincentville for twelve years. The work has been hard and uncompromising; his children have been isolated in the mostly Mormon community, and he has been viewed with suspicion. But Ron Anthony had come to Vincentville "to stay."

Many of those who attended the little frame church on the outskirts of Vincentville were construction workers from the South who were building a large federal installation nearby.

Anthony has been active in community affairs and frequently is seen visiting and working in the town. Still, he did not fully gain acceptance. The breakthrough came when a tornado ripped through the town, damaging hundreds of homes and leaving several thousand people homeless. He began to minister to Mormon and non-Mormon alike. He got help from his denomination and was tireless in his efforts.

*It was a long wait, but a natural disaster finally brought accep-
tance to the pastor who came to Vincentville "to stay."*

Church planting is hard work. Often it is frustrating and unreward-
ing. Many times breakthroughs are long in coming and response
is slow.

Workers who are involved in church planting must be patient
and highly motivated.

Motivation is essential. Costs often are high and always an enor-
mous amount of time is required on the part of the church planter.
Forty-hour weeks will never get churches planted nor will just going
to meetings. Church planting is endless, tiresome, demanding, and
extremely hard.

Pastors who set their sights on twenty calls a week will not succeed—sixty or more are required. Evangelistic and ministry visits
demand a high output of emotional energy on the part of the worker.

Committed workers are needed at all stages of church development. Many diverse talents are needed, and these need to be motivated to respond and serve. The sponsoring church needs to be
committed to the project.

Church planting calls for sacrifice in giving, in prayer, and in
service. New churches will not be established without this output
of effort and dedication. To succeed, churches and church planters
must be able to see—and to feel—the need, to be convinced that
something can be done to meet the need, and that they can do
something about that need.

• Flexibility Is Crucial in Church Planting

*Norman Abbott was a successful pastor in Carson. It was a univer-
sity town, and Abbott retained a professor from the college to direct
the music. The musical program was stately, with an eighty-voice
choir, mostly trained voices. The organist was skilled in Bach, Bee-
thoven, and Mendelssohn.*

*The people in the church responded favorably to the music, which
set the stage for the stately, classical, majestic services in the huge,
white-columned sanctuary.*

*Abbott was called to a church in Kelray. He had been successful
in setting the musical stage for the worship experience with the
classical-style music; he thought it would work again. He retained*

a trained musical director and gave instructions for the impressive music.

Attendance lagged, and the worship services were a bore. Abbott examined the church and found that the socioeconomic, cultural, and educational level indicated the people would respond better to a different style of worship. He installed a piano and bought some paperback, gospel songbooks. The music leader moved to a spirited, gospel song service on Sunday morning. Abbott began to preach in a less restrained manner.

As a result, the church was overflowing with people who had a joyous, vigorous worship experience.

Flexibility is the key to church activity. What works in one church will not always work in another. Flexibility does not indicate a change in theology, just a change in the methodology. The truths are the same, but the styles of presentation must be flexible to meet the needs of the moment.

Every facet of church planting activity needs to always be open to scrutiny. Nothing is set in granite.

We must be flexible in worship styles. Some communities respond well to printed bulletins, while others react adversely to such "formality." Some like stately hymns and classical organ preludes, while others like peppy gospel songs.

We must be flexible in building styles. Church buildings should fit the life-style of the community. Ornate, classical structures are out of place in simple, working-class communities. Similarly, store-front churches are not in keeping with higher socioeconomic neighborhoods.

We must be flexible in church programming. What appeals to a university community may evoke no interest or response at all in a working-class area or in a nonacademic, middle-class section.

We must be flexible in church activities. There may be no need for a ministry to older adults in a community populated by young married couples, and there may be no need for a nursery in a church located in a senior-citizen community.

Flexibility is the key. The Holy Spirit will lead as we seek the style of worship, ministry, building, program, and activity for our individual church.

In 1 Corinthians, Paul talks of the ultimate in flexibility when he says he will not be bound by his background of Hebraic customs but has "become all things to all men, that I might by all means save some" (9:22).

• We Must Build Bridges to People in Effective Church Planting

Marshall Keyes became pastor of Northvale Church in a growing suburb. He had been the pastor of a small church in the mountains of an Eastern state and the only method of reaching people he knew was knocking on doors.

Keyes went door to door in a large apartment house and kept getting thrown out. But he kept right on trying. One night he was knocking on a door and a young girl answered.

"Hello. I am Marshall Keyes, pastor of Northvale Church. Where do you go to church?" he started. The girl just grinned at him. He repeated his introduction and she grinned a little wider. He started a third time when the girl's brother appeared.

"She doesn't speak any English," the young man said, himself speaking in broken English.

Keyes was dumbfounded. He stood there collecting his thoughts and heard himself saying, "I'm trying to tell her that we are going to have a class at our church this Thursday night on how to speak English." Keyes admits he doesn't know why he said it, and chalks it up to the fact that the Holy Spirit knew of the need and got involved.

The brother grinned widely and replied, "Well, there will be four of us there."

Keyes had three days to figure out how he would have the language classes. He did, and in three months, 140 people were involved in the literacy work.

Marshall Keyes found a need and built a bridge between Northvale Church and the community in order to meet the need and to present Jesus Christ to the people who came.

If we want to build churches anywhere in this world, we must build bridges to people. We must open avenues of approach. Christian churches must figure ways to meet needs, to identify an interest or a need, and to build a bridge of approach. Churches must become a friend of the community.

We will not reach people if we go in with a chip on our shoulder, proclaiming we are the only church with the gospel or professing that we are going to teach those "liberals" how to preach. We reach people by becoming friends with them, by meeting a need, or by becoming involved in an area of interest.

There are many ways to build bridges. Literacy classes such as the one Marshall Keyes started is one way. Others include—and the list is not exhaustive—recreation programs, day-care centers, well-baby clinics, cooking classes, sewing and knitting classes, coaching, tutoring, senior-citizens programs, financial counseling.

A bridge has been built when you've met a need. Building bridges does not mean we have to compromise ourselves, but it does mean that we have to give ourselves in love and concern. Building bridges says "WE CARE" to the people who are around us.

3. The Practical Foundations

● **Church Planting Is Primarily the Task of a Local Church**

Charles Rhodenbush is a member of First Church in Burlington. He is active and serving as a deacon, a Sunday School outreach leader, and a program leader for the men's group.

One of the programs for the men's meeting was a discussion on planned parenthood for churches. The lesson discussed means of determining whether a new church is needed, and ways of going about planting one.

The group, under Rhodenbush's leadership, became excited about the possibilities. They asked their pastor, Bill Conners, to investigate. He checked and found a rapidly growing area about ten miles from the church. The section—like most of Florida—is booming. Included were more than 600 permanent residences and some 1,000 mobile homes. The area was more than five miles from the nearest church of any kind.

The men began to survey the area. They were unable to find a meeting place, so they arranged the purchase of five acres of land and built a small building. Services were started.

As the mission began, Pastor Conners asked members of the church to fill out a questionnaire indicating their willingness to go to the mission to form the nucleus. When the mission started, the church commissioned and sent the chairman of the deacons, two other deacons, two Sunday School outreach leaders, the direc-tor of the women's group, a licensed preacher, and an ordained preacher. It sent twenty-five of its key people to start the new work.

In the two years since the mission began, the church and mission have seen ninety-one professions of faith and more than 100 other additions. Enrollment and attendance have climbed, as have financial contributions.

"We have been in a continuous revival since we began the mission," says Pastor Conners with a big smile on his face.

Church planting is a normal and natural function for a church. If it does not take on this task, it has become rootbound. The early church set aside workers to go out and establish new churches. Modern congregations might copy the pattern and provide support and undergird the effort with prayer.

Church planting is a task of the local church. This is based on Scripture. Also, it is a more practical, efficient, and effective way than any other system.

Thousands of local congregations can see the needy communities around them much better than can a few workers in a national or regional denominational office. More needs are seen if local congregations are sensitized to the responsibility they bear in starting new work. Local churches also can give far better supervision to a mission project, to administering funds, and to volunteer workers than can a far distant denominational office.

Local churches which involve themselves in church planting often have great revivals break out in their own congregations as a result of the spiritual blessings of being involved in mission outreach work. It happened at First Church; it can happen elsewhere too.

• There Must Be Committed Human Leaders for Effective Church Planting

Larry Elliott was the fourth pastor in four years to pastor Newland Church in one of our Western states. The other pastors had become tired of the daily struggle and had been "called" to more prosperous churches or more promising areas.

Elliott came to the church as a bi-vocational pastor, working during the daytime as a repairman and laboring as pastor of the small church in the evenings and on weekends.

It was a struggle for Elliott, his wife, Bernice, and their three sons. The work was hard, the hours long, and the results often disappointing.

But he stayed and loved the people of Newland Church. He visited without fail, and when there was a need, he was always there. He preached simple, short, and well-prepared sermons, although the people sometimes had wondered when Elliott had the time to get them ready.

The field was hard, but Elliott stayed on. Gradually the mission began to grow, attracting families from the town and surrounding ranches. Elliott trained the people to witness and to take responsibility. Soon, he had help in his visitation, and growth was faster.

Because of his commitment, Larry Elliott built a church where four other men had failed. He was effective because he stuck to it and just kept working.

New churches must have committed human leadership. The leaders—including pastor and people—must work hard and long to build the church. They are the "stackpole people" around whom the church is built.

The leadership must not depend entirely on the pastor, or the mission might crumble if he moved away. The leadership should be diversified to include lay persons who are steady and dependable. They are the persons around whom the church is built.

A pastor in Chicago refers to such leadership people as "heart families." And it is around these "heart families" that mission congregations are firmly established.

• Priorities Must Be Defined for Effective Church Planting

I was pastor of a small mission church in Colorado Springs and learned firsthand what it means to define priorities. The congregation was small and the needs were many. I spent a day each week cutting the stencil and mimeographing the Sunday bulletin.

Then, I launched an intensive teacher-training program which required extensive record-keeping for appropriate awards and recognition. I found myself involved in spending about a day each week keeping the records and requesting awards.

The congregation was on a main artery of Colorado Springs, so we had frequent visitors in our worship services. As a means of contact with the visitors, I started a weekly mail-out bulletin to all visitors and members.

Suddenly it dawned on me that I was spending three days each week on paperwork. I found a volunteer for the bulletin, another for the midweek mail out, and a third to serve as training secretary.

My time was eaten up doing things which should have been of low priority. With the three volunteers, I was able to do things which had a higher priority: evangelistic visitation and sermon preparation.

In the book of Acts, Luke records that the apostles became so bogged down in detail work that they had no time to do the things they should have been doing. They got the people together and elected seven deacons to take over serving the tables, freeing them to "devote ourselves to prayer and to the ministry of the word" (Acts 6:4, RSV).

There are many areas of work in church planting which must be ranked according to priority. Order of importance must be given to such things as places where new churches are needed, emphases in programming, expenditure of funds, utilization of workers, use of the pastor's time, and many other things. Priorities should be based on the degree of need and the available resources to meet those needs.

First, priority should be given to identifying places where churches are needed and then establishing the degree of need in each place. (A system of selecting areas for new churches will be suggested in Section II of this book.)

Once a church-planting project is launched, most new church situations fail to establish priorities about church programs and use of the pastor's time.

Church programming should start with the Bible and the first convert, moving on to a fully age-graded Sunday School, followed by a worship experience. When a nucleus of believers is gathered, a program of training and development should be started. The growth of the program and its format should progress in keeping with the number of persons available and the intensity of need.

For instance, a fourteen-member church doesn't need a full "five-star" program. Such a program requires more manpower than is available, and each person will have four or five jobs. They'll be so busy running around keeping the machinery going that they won't have time to visit prospects.

The other area of failure to establish priorities is in the use of the pastor's time. The mission pastor sometimes is so bogged down in detail that he cannot extricate himself. He fritters away his time on useless busywork and fails to reach the lost and unchurched.

If there is no volunteer to produce a Sunday bulletin, the church should do without one, especially if the pastor's time would be absorbed in doing it. He can spend his time more usefully preparing his sermons and doing evangelistic visitation.

Failure to set priorities often results in lack of accomplishment.

- **Participation Planning on All Levels Is Essential for Effective Church Planting**

One last word on church-planting foundations: the entire sponsoring congregation should be involved in planning for the church-planting project. The church missions committee (discussed in Section II) must keep the membership notified.

Further, to be effective, regional, state, and national denominational offices should have a part in planning the new mission congregation.

Such total involvement insures a more efficient and stable church planting effort.

SECTION II

The Nine Steps of Church Planting

1. Select a church missions committee.
2. Select areas for new work.
3. Prepare the sponsoring church.
4. Cultivate the field.
5. Establish the mission fellowship.
6. Establish the mission chapel.
7. Deal with financial issues.
8. Provide facilities for the mission chapel.
9. Constitute the chapel into a church.

4. Select a Church Missions Committee (Step One)

Trinity Church, in a poorly attended Wednesday night business meeting, voted to become the sponsor of Westside Mission. There was little discussion even though the decision to sponsor the mission included some financial and personal responsibilities on the part of Trinity. They only did it because Howard Large, the director of missions, had asked them to.

Trinity provided $250 per month, an action that was regularly approved by the deacons and by the congregation at the business meeting. Most of the 1,000 members of Trinity would have been surprised if they had known the church was sponsoring a mission. There was never a mention of the mission in the church newsletter, in the Sunday bulletin, in Sunday School, or from the pulpit. The only notice was a single line in the financial statement, buried alongside telephone bills, maintenance costs, salaries for the church staff, and payments on the church's new riding lawnmower.

Westside Mission, established in a rapidly growing section of town, met in the auditorium of Westside Elementary School. There were many problems and needs, but when mission leaders took their problems to their "sponsor," they were met with disinterest and found there was no responsible person or group in the church to help them.

After struggling along for more than a year, Westside had to suspend operations. Most of those who had been involved in the mission were sad. They could see vast areas on the west side of town where a gospel witness was needed. But, when they needed help, their "sponsor" could not relate to them or help them with their problems.

Many church-type missions have endured agony—and many have died—because the mother church was not properly geared to relate actively to its mission congregation. In situations where relating to the mission congregations is nobody's specific business, it becomes everybody's business, and the old adage of "everybody's business is nobody's business" is still true. Many of the missions which have died were in areas of great need and great potential, but they simply could not make it on their own.

Many churches involved in beginning new congregations have found a small competent group—usually called the church missions committee—to be the best way to relate to the mission congregations. It is their business and their responsibility to work with the missions.

Many new churches have been sponsored by churches who simply voted to sponsor, to "extend an arm" for membership and the ordinances. The work was done by one or two interested persons. In those cases, when problems arise in the mission congregation, there is no knowledgeable group to handle them on behalf of the church. If mission problems are tossed into the lap of the deacons without research and without facts, poor decisions may be made. Further, without a planning and administering group, like the church missions committee, the sponsoring church misses the blessing of total church involvement in the mission project. Such total involvement often sparks a revival in the sponsoring church; lack of involvement, on the other hand, often causes division and dissension, as rumors circulate and speculations abound.

Mission problems, ignored by the sponsoring congregation, sometimes have intensified to the point that the mission died. Annually, Southern Baptists start nearly twice as many church-type missions as are constituted into churches. There is a lot of fall out. Research indicates the presence of a properly functioning church missions committee could have guaranteed the success of many mission congregations.

The church missions committee has been called the missions conscience of the church. Perhaps it could more correctly be called the catalyst for missions. A chief task of the committee is to make studies to determine mission needs. After the needs are discovered, the committee assigns priorities, analyzes resources, and brings the needs, priorities, and resources before the church.

In the case of starting new work, the committee normally has the responsibility to do the nitty-gritty, detail work which should precede any beginning. The group generally carries through with responsibilities for launching the new mission and then continues to relate to the needs and problems of the new congregation as it grows.

The Task of the Church Missions Committee in Starting New Churches

One of the principle functions of the church missions committee is to create a climate in the mother church that is conducive to beginning new work. One of the principle roadblocks in the way of churches sponsoring missions is the absence in the church of a suitable climate—openness, interest, concern. The committee is needed initially to deal with this lack of interest and concern.

Church missionary organizations do much to create a general missions climate, but most churches are lacking motivation when it comes to starting new churches in a neighboring or nearby community. Frequently, the lack of motivation comes from lack of information about specific needs in a specific area. Missions, when presented in the huge nebulous "out there" creates a general impression but no specific target.

A carefully prepared plan to create an awareness of specific new church needs in a specific area must be developed, using all organizations and services of the church to implement it. A constant flow of missions information should be channeled to church membership through every means available.

To be effective, the information should clearly present the need, convincing the congregation that something can be done to meet the need and that the individual congregation can do something to meet the need.

Another task of the church missions committe is identifying needs for new churches. The committee should accumulate data about communities or neighborhoods which need a new church. The data must be studied and interpreted, and priorities must be established. Such data is readily available from the chamber of commerce, bank planning departments, city or county planning commissions, or from the regional denominational organization. Other material is available from census publications, community agencies, interchurch offices, and social welfare departments.

Recently, Faith Church in Croxton began to research its community. When the data had been assembled and interpreted, members went to the community planning council. The church leaders were surprised to find they had more data—and more accurate information—than did the governmental body! They were asked to share their research with the council.

After completing its research, the church missions committee should present its facts to church leadership. A carefully organized presentation must be prepared so the church and its leaders can readily and easily grasp the implications with a minimum of explanation. The committee should report its findings to the church council or deacons for reaction and input and then to the total church family.

After a church votes to sponsor a church-type mission, it should assign administrative responsibility for the project to the committee for ongoing direction and implementation. After the project is launched, the committee will be responsible for nurturing the infant congregation until it can stand alone as a church in its own right.

The committee should hold at least one meeting each month, at which the mission congregation may submit reports, discuss problems and needs, and receive feedback from the mother church. Dangers of embarrassing and unauthorized activities can be avoided if proper relationships are established and maintained. Preventive maintenance in starting new missions is much more effective than is crisis management.

The meetings offer a great time for spiritual encouragement of both the sponsor and the mission. The meeting offers a good forum for greater support and communication between the fledgling congregation and its sponsoring organization.

Selection of the Church Missions Committee

Members of the church missions committee must be carefully chosen. The committee should be composed of capable church members who are respected by their brethren. The members should be recommended by the nominating committee and elected by the church.

Characteristics desired in the committee members include these:
- Missionary minded
- Spiritually minded
- Concerned about people
- Able to gather and analyze data

- Able to work with people
- Willing to work
- Capable of leadership
- Warm, loving, caring people
- Optimistic in spirit

The committee should have three to seven members, depending on the size of the church. They should be elected from the church membership at large, but should include representatives from women's, men's, and Sunday School organizations. It should have at least two officers, a chairperson, and a secretary.

Members of the committee also must be carefully—thoroughly and adequately—trained to enable them to perform their jobs in leading in a church development project.

Initial training may begin as members are provided material to read relating to the mission of the church, including the biblical basis of church planting. The books may be circulated and then discussed in home fellowship meetings, establishing a solid foundation of missions concepts and understandings upon which to build missions methodology.

Study sessions should be scheduled for the committee to work through manuals and guidebooks relating to starting new churches. Filmstrips and movies are available, and often a speaker can be secured from regional or state denominational offices. Committee retreats also are effective ways to prepare members for their work.

Long before the committee attempts to lead the church in an outreach project, the committee should thoroughly train itself in its job.

Other training opportunities are available. Often, two or three churches may coordinate training of the individual committees for greater effectiveness. The local or regional denominational organization may conduct a Church Missions Committee Workshop for the entire region. State and national conferences are offered periodically, and the church should attempt to send its chairperson or another member of the committee to enlarge the vision.

Every effort should be made to keep a continuing training process going for members of the committee, updating experienced members and orienting new members.

However, the committee should never become so immersed in training that it forgets what the training is equipping it to do.

Operation of the Church Missions Committee

The committee should meet monthly and have called meetings as needs arise. Representatives from the mission congregation should attend the monthly meetings, presenting reports and making known any problems in the fledgling church. The committee should listen closely, asking questions and seeking to get the complete picture. Any matter needing approval from the sponsoring church should go as a recommendation from the church missions committee, not as a direct request from the mission congregation.

The committee, as it works in new church development, should relate to all organizations of the church. The Sunday School should be enlisted to assist with development of the Bible-teaching program of the new congregation. Mission organizations should assist with mission ministry projects and should provide volunteers for special projects. The training program should train new converts—both at the mother church and at the mission—in the faith. The music ministry of the sponsor should seek to provide music talent to the congregation. Correlation of program involvements normally should be through the church council, in consultation with the church missions committee.

The church missions committee should have some meetings devoted solely to planning to meet other new church needs which have been discovered through research and study. Gathering data should be an ongoing process for the committee. Other opportunities for planting other mission congregations should be developed and organized for presentation to the church through the council and deacon body.

In its meetings, the church missions committee occasionally should invite the chairman of the associational missions committee or the associational director of missions to meet with them. These regional leaders often have insight that assists greatly as the committee plans and implements its work.

5. Select Areas for New Work (Step Two)

"I guess we just picked the wrong place to begin," Pastor John Long told associational director of missions Truett Johnson. "Somehow, it just didn't work out. . . ."

As Long talked with Johnson, men from Main Street Church loaded pews, pulpit, piano, and other furnishings on pickup trucks. Other men worked to board up the windows and doors of the small building to prevent vandalism.

Main Street Church had worked for four years to give birth to Center Hill chapel. It had been a struggle, as membership and giving declined. Finally, it just dwindled to almost nothing.

Main Street Church had not used good judgment in selecting a site for the chapel. The section where they attempted to plant Center Hill was fast becoming an industrial area. Light industry, warehouses, and small businesses had moved into the area. As they moved in, the residential areas changed. A new superhighway was built across the area, bisecting it, and closing off the area which was still residential.

Because of lack of community response—and, in fact, because few people were left—Center Hill died.

Southern Baptists annually close about one third of their "new mission starts." Only about two thirds ever grow to congregation status. Too many do not survive.

Failure to obtain full and complete facts on a neighborhood or community prior to launching a new congregation may be just like signing the death warrant long before the new work has been started. Thousands of dollars of missions funds have been poured into pastoral support in new church situations which often took five, ten, or fifteen years to take root and grow. Many times the slowness to take root has been simply because the choice of neighborhood was not the best. Occasionally, after years of struggle, a mission congregation will relocate to a new area where growth suddenly takes place.

Good stewardship of funds, personnel, and time dictates that a full and careful investigation be made before anything is started. To do otherwise is folly, no matter how good a site or situation may look after a cursory glance.

Criteria to Consider in Selecting Sites for Strategic New Churches

When considering locations for new churches, sponsoring churches or regional denominational organizations should ask a series of questions. The questions will provide sponsors with information on whether they can locate churches in the area and whether the new churches will become a great reservoir of strength and support in developing a total missions program for the region.

Does the area have a great unmet need for the ministry and witness of a new church? Are there a disproportionate number of unchurched people? Are existing churches failing to present an effective gospel witness? Are existing churches failing to minister adequately to the needs of the people in the community?

An Example: When church planter Alfred Logan looked at Washington Township, all he saw was church steeples. They seemed to be everywhere. Tall, squat, pretty, ugly, white, copper; they were all over the town of 35,000.

He thought the prospects looked pretty unpromising, but he decided to do a survey anyway. Census data revealed—through simple division—there was one church for every 1,700 people in the community. He persisted, taking a community survey aided by the missions committee from Jefferson in an adjoining county. The survey uncovered some surprising facts. Despite the fact that Washington Township was heavily churched, more than 85 percent of the people neither attended church nor claimed membership in any church. A huge portion of the population was unchurched. Somehow, the existing churches were not making an impact on the county.

As a result, the Jefferson church sponsored a mission in Washington Township. Despite the number of churches in the community, Washington Township had a great unmet need for the ministry and witness of a new church.

Can a new church in this area wield a strong influence for God that will reach out effectively into the surrounding area? Will a church in this area become a base of outreach over a large area of the region?

An Example: Midvale Church was located in the midst of densely populated Reagan County. It started with only a handful of people. The outreach was small as it ministered to a small pocket of people.

But, as it grew, a program of multiple ministries was established. Hundreds of lives were touched through literacy programs, social-action work, ministries to youth, families, and the elderly. As needs were established, ministries were started to help meet them. Bridges were built into the community—bridges of care and love and trust.

Along the way, as Midvale grew, she also reached out to start new work—new mission congregations—in other areas of Reagan county. Initially, these were home fellowship missions led by Midvale laypersons. One soon grew to a "Wednesday school and worship" with Pastor Dale Smith bringing the message each Wednesday night to a sizable crowd. The group constituted into a mission and then into a congregation.

In six years, Midvale started and sponsored eight mission congregations, expanding the witness and ministry of the church into Reagan County.

Midvale, which started with a tiny handful, exerted strong influence for God that reached effectively into the surrounding area.

Can a new church minister to people who will convey the impact of its message to other parts of the nation and the world? Is this the sort of community—like a major academic or industrial center— where people can be won, trained, and sent as emissaries of the gospel to the whole world?

An Example: Park Street Church was started in a small—in fact, tiny—house near the campus of State University. The university has worldwide fame, with excellent training, research, and academic programs. People came from around the world to attend. Its graduates are leaders in their professions around the globe.

Park Street Church struggled and struggled to keep the spark of life alive. The university was renowned, but the little church was obscure. In time, denominational assistance was given so the congregation could launch an aggressive program with a resident pastor. Elbert Bridges, a man of unique abilities, was called to minister in the university setting. The little church literally exploded with growth. The congregation built two lovely buildings and attained strength to become self-supporting.

But, most importantly, the church reached key people who were receiving training at the university. Today, alumni of the church—people who accepted Jesus Christ as their personal Savior under the love and care of Park Street Church—girdle the globe. People from all sections of the nation, as well as Asia, Africa, Europe, South and Central America, were won to Christ and discipled at Park Street. Today, because the church was planted and flourished there, its witness is extended almost beyond measure.

Park Street ministered to people who conveyed the impact of its message to other parts of the nation and the world.

Does this area have sufficient growth potential to develop a church that will become strong enough to do these things effectively? Is there an adequate number of people—many with leadership potential—who possess the intellectual ability and resourcefulness to give this new church great leadership in becoming a truly great church?

An Example: Immanuel Church was in a densely populated area of a large Western city. It achieved strength rather rapidly and proceeded on an ambitious new church-development program. In seven years, it started a dozen new churches. As the number of new units multiplied, effectiveness in outreach and ministry also was multiplied. Vast numbers of people were reached through the new units, far more than Immanuel could ever have reached alone.

As its witness expanded through the new units, Immanuel also grew at home, tripling its own membership and attendance.

Criteria to Consider in Adequately Churching an Area for Religious Coverage

A series of questions should be asked when considering whether an area is adequately churched for total religious coverage.

Do the existing churches adequately represent evangelical Christianity for the effective evangelistic penetration of the community? Are there other Southern Baptist churches, other kinds of Baptist churches, Bible churches, and conservative congregations of mainline denominations in the community?

An Example: In Conklin the Protestant congregations were either far left or far right in theology. The pastor of the leading First Church did not believe in the virgin birth of Christ, the miracles of Christ, or the Genesis account of the creation. On the other end of the spectrum was True Vine Church which accepted only the King James Version of the Bible and maintained that only people who were baptized in their group were saved.

One conservative evangelical group made a study of the community of Acton and found the only evangelical presence in town was two ultrafundamental churches. Again, the mainstream of American Protestant Christianity was absent.

In both Acton and Conklin, new churches were started, reflecting a "middle-ground" theology. Both received good response, and both have grown extremely well.

Is the strength, mission involvement, and spiritual climate of the existing evangelical churches sufficient for them to give an adequate and effective witness in the community? Can the churches, with existing conditions, reputations, and membership, reach the unchurched?

An Example: In Beaverton, there were two churches of the same evangelical conservative faith: First Church and Beaverton Church.

First Church had an unenviable record of continually forcing its pastors to resign. In ten years they had six pastors. The tactics were gossip, innuendo, and other unchristian acts toward the minister and his family. One favorite tactic was to withhold tithes to "starve him out."

Beaverton Church was unruly. Frequent controversies erupted in business meetings. Once, police had to be called. There were several factions, all struggling to get control of the little church.

There was a heavy flow of transfers of membership from one church to the other. Members frequently transferred to the opposite church after an argument, fight, or problem. The condition went on for years.

From outward appearances, it appeared the town had a fine witness and ministry. Closer examination revealed that the internal problems made the existing churches nothing but a hull without content.

A third church—Grace Church—was added and blossomed rapidly. Leadership worked to keep it free of strife and confusion. It avoided the problems which plagued the other congregations.

As a further note, coldness and lethargy might account for a failure to witness adequately to the community. In one county seat of

350,000, the first and only church representing a major evangelical denomination went for three years without any professions of faith, yet over 75 percent of the people in the county were unchurched. The church was uninterested in any form of evangelism and had neither mission outreach nor community ministry.

Is the statistical evangelistic record of existing churches for the past five years indicative that they are really making an effective penetration of the unchurched? What does the statistical data reflect about the growth of existing churches, including Sunday School attendance, baptismal additions, additions by transfer, worship attendance, giving, and other such items? Do members of the church live in the community?

An Example: A major evangelical denomination undertook an intensive study of its churches in a major metropolitan area of the nation. The study revealed a decline in baptisms, membership, attendance, and giving in the number of churches in the area over the period studied. The denomination definitely believes in evangelism—as did the churches studied. Somehow, however, they just weren't getting the job done.

When existing churches plateau and become stagnant or go into decline, the only effective alternative is to start new churches to reverse the trend. Not many old churches are able to change their style in order to reach the community effectively.

Are existing churches representative of the socioeconomic and cultural spread of the community? Are all segments of the community reflected in the churches which exist there? Do styles of worship, preaching, and music appeal to the cultural tastes of the population? What is the educational level and how is it reflected in the church program? Are there language or ethnic groups in the community who do not have a church of their own language or culture to attend?

An Example: In Salem, a new church was started two blocks from a sister church. The years passed and both congregations grew effectively.

When Don Roberts came to the newer congregation, he was troubled by the geographical proximity of one church to the other. He had been taught that no church of a denomination should be closer than one mile from a sister church.

Roberts asked the denominational leader of the area if he should seek to move the church, relocating it at a more respectable distance from the other congregation.

"No, you are ministering to two entirely different strata of society. You are reaching people who wouldn't go over there, and they are touching people who wouldn't come to your church. The styles of worship and ministry are altogether different," the denominational leader told him.

In order to reach the community—in all its strata—multiple churches of the same faith, beamed to different socioeconomic and cultural groups, are essential.

Do existing churches adequately minister to the physical, social, emotional, and spiritual needs of the people in the community? Do the churches show love and care? Are they reaching out to minister to the hurts, hopes, and beings of the people who live there?

An Example: First Church of Bloomingdale had been on the street corner near the downtown section for a long time. Its red brick walls were covered with ivy and the church plant took up a half block.

But, inside the church, the members were those who drove from other sections, intent on holding on to their old "home church." As they came to worship, they drove by transitional communities and areas which had changed from being the better to the worst sections of town.

The people rode in locked cars, looking with distrust at the people in the apartments, in ramshackle houses, and on the trash-littered streets.

The church and its members cared about "what used to be" rather than "what is now." They feared and disliked the people who lived around the church. The church dwindled to a faithful few who clung to their old "home church."

Kelley Maxwell came to be pastor of the church. He worked to break the pattern, but it was too ingrained. Changing course, he led the church to consider ministering to the people of the community by starting a new work. With some wealth and power left, the congregation financed the mission. It blossomed as it offered ministries and worship which touched the hearts of the people who lived in the new ghetto.

Failure to minister to the hurts of the community sometimes is adequate reason to enter a community with a new, ministering church.

Do the statistics on the numbers of unchurched persons reflect an adequate challenge to start a new church?

An Example: Fellowship Church was established on the outskirts of Madison. It was formed of people who had received a "new touch from the Lord."

At first, Fellowship grew rapidly, and the members reveled in the new members. However, an analysis of the new members showed most of them were coming by transfer of letters or by statement from other Protestant churches in Madison.

Before long, the word got around that the members of the church were proselyting members elsewhere. Fellowship had little evangelical outreach but was founded on stealing members away from other churches.

New congregations ought to enter a community beamed to the unchurched, not with the perspective of proselyting members from existing churches. The numbers of unchurched people in America— an estimated 150 million out of a total population of 218 million— are an adequate challenge without spinning our wheels picking at fellow-professing Christians of other persuasions. A dependable survey to determine the number of unchurched people is a must.

Does the ratio of community-population growth to church-membership growth reveal that existing churches are not amalgamating new residents into the fellowship of their churches? Is population growing at a faster rate than the church membership of the existing churches?

An Example: Oxford is a small town in the southern United States. In 1965 it had a sleepy, stable population of 4,500. However, Oxford is in the sunbelt, and two major corporations moved manufacturing and office facilities to Oxford, swelling the population to more than 12,000 in ten years.

Denominational leaders made a survey of overall church membership and found, astonishingly, that the additional 7,500 people made no difference at all in church membership. The churches rocked along as if the town still had 4,500 people. The program worship style, outreach, and ministry had not significantly changed since Oxford was a sleepy, little village where everybody knew everybody else.

The story of Oxford can be documented time and again across our nation. Generally, new residents require new churches if they are going to be effectively reached and ministered to.

Surveying the Community to Determine the Site for a New Church

Initially, a survey is not intended to determine the exact street corner where the new church should be, but to determine the area location for a new church.

Location determination for a new church should follow this sequence:

* Town or city is determined.
* Section or region of the city or town is determined.
* Neighborhood is determined.
* Exact site is chosen.

Determine the town or city where a church will be located.

A look at the census data is the initial step in making selection of the town or city. The data which contains the total population of the city also reveals such information as age, race, types of employment, educational level, types of homes, language, and similar material. The use of a community-profile form (Appendix A) will be helpful in organizing the data.

Serious probing into the religious life of the community is a must for an intelligent decision about whether or not to enter the city. Material can be obtained by telephoning pastors, making personal visits, or through asking tactful questions. Such information as kind and number of churches, membership, and average attendance is critical.

A "sampling survey" of homes with religious survey cards may also be advisable. A telephone survey or random house-to-house survey will be helpful.

Determine the section of a city or town.

Occasionally, in gathering religious data, friendly conversations with pastors of existing churches will reveal a vacuum for a particular kind of church in a specific section of the city or town. This is one of the best reasons for an intensive religious probe as outlined above.

Several steps should be taken before making any door-to-door survey or telephone survey.

First, the area being considered should be clearly marked on a map of the city or town to avoid needless duplication of effort in the future. Care should be taken to keep the area in manageable proportions and to be aware of geographical boundaries which limit neighborhoods and church growth. Marking the boundaries also will aid future planning for the area.

A noncopyrighted map, which can be reproduced without permission, is usually obtainable at the chamber of commerce, state highway department, or planning commission. Major future changes— interstate highways, urban renewal projects, industrial developments, parks, and the like—should be marked. Other community elements also should be marked—rivers, roads, highways, streets, parks, golf courses, cemeteries, business and commercial areas, industrial areas, residential sections, and railroads. Such natural boundaries often limit neighborhoods and the potential for church growth.

Second, existing churches should be marked, with separate symbols representing the various denominations. This helps indicate the dispersal of the churches. Denominational symbols show at a glance the location of churches of like faith and practice, as well as those of similar belief.

Third, economic conditions of the city or town should be studied. Use of the Church Extension Community Analysis form (Appendix B) will help identify the specific economic data to seek out, such as number of industries in the area, the leading industry, type of labor which is predominant, the unemployment rate, and prospects for new industry.

Fourth, social characteristics such as mobility, cultural levels, educational levels, ethnic makeup of the population, racial groups, types of housing available, radio stations getting the heaviest listenership, types of cars, and club memberships should be studied.

Fifth, population data from the census reports should be studied. This data gives information concerning the housing, age structure, and ethnic and racial percentages. Population changes between the last two decennial censuses give information of mobility, growth, decrease, or change. City or county planning commissions are usually glad to be helpful to church groups planning new congregations because such new developments help them in implementing some of their dreams for the community.

An Example: Bethany Church was started in Bellville. It grew rather rapidly until it had over 100 in attendance. Members purchased a huge site for a large sum then issued a bond issue far beyond its ability to pay. Members counted on the growth rate continuing. It was sort of an ecclesiastical parley.

Because of the indebtedness, the church floundered and failed. It died in debt and disgrace. A study after the fact showed only six new homes had been built in the county in the past five years. Population was very static. There were large numbers of unchurched people in the county, but long-term residents tend to be slower in changing church affiliation. Bethany could have lived if it had studied community data and learned more about its own community before taking the huge leap into debt.

Sixth, if all of the initial data looks encouraging, some sort of religious census or survey should be taken to get more specific data and to help pinpoint a specific neighborhood for the ultimate location. Family survey cards can be obtained from any religious bookstore. They may be used for a door-to-door effort or for a telephone survey, using a street directory of the neighborhood. (Chapter 7 gives more detailed data on surveys.)

Several denominations might work together on such a survey, securing better community response and reducing the workload on the new group attempting to start the work.

Determine the neighborhood.

Selecting the particular neighborhood in a city or town may take longer than it took to select the community or the section of the community.

From survey data cultivative activities may begin. As friends are made, as people make decisions, as small fellowship groups are formed, the neighborhood will begin to surface. The door-to-door survey data coupled with earlier research and personal response from the people will usually bring the exact neighborhood into focus.

Determine the site for a new church.

The urgency of site selection will vary from place to place. In an exploding development, site acquisition should be done early or the price may become astronomical. In these cases, church and denominational leaders need to work far in advance in order to buy available property.

Across the nation, however, most communities are slow moving enough that the nucleus can come together in a home fellowship or temporary meeting place for sometime prior to selecting land. If time permits in the property market in the area, it is best to let the new congregation make its own site selection. Often when the sponsoring church purchases property for the new congregation, the effect is much like that of parents of a newlywed couple buying a home without consultation with the young people. It can boomerang badly.

Often, it is difficult to get a mission congregation to assume the burden of property which was not of their choosing. However, mission congregations show excitement in the purchasing and building of a church home when they make the plans and decisions relative to the purchase.

General Considerations in Selecting Areas for New Churches

Church planting workers should be aware of the various agencies which can be helpful in many ways. Some already have been mentioned. These are the research and planning offices of the local council or federation of churches; city, county, or regional planning commissions; local, district, or regional offices of their denomination; state or national mission offices responsible for church extension.

Another consideration is that a great number of "pocket" communities will need expressions of church, and the church-type missions there generally will be slow to come to self-support. Some may never be able to support themselves. However, these are some of the neediest communities in the world. Church missions committees should, in many cases, select these areas of need and implement extension congregations there. Many of these are blighted areas in the city or are desolate rural or small town neighborhoods.

A recent article in the *New York Times* indicates community leaders and governmental agencies feel that storefront churches in the blighted areas of the city have given cohesion and stability to the community, as well as enhancing chances of a comeback. Of course, the reason for the good community effect is that people find Christ, and their life-style then changes for the better.

A Final Thought

After massing all the data suggested in this chapter and after considering all the criteria indicated, the church missions committee members will be better able to make intelligent, spiritual commitments.

They also will be better equipped to lead their church to accept a new church extension project as a means of evangelistic penetration into an unchurched community and then to bring the ministry of that church to those in need.

6. Prepare the Sponsoring Church (Step Three)

When I was a pastor, the churches I served began many mission congregations. Usually that happened because I saw the need, enlisted a leader, and launched the mission chapel. Generally, when I left the church, the mission extension died. That was because it was a pastor's mission.

Later, when I was a regional director of missions, I also led in starting many missions. Again, it happened most frequently because I saw the need, found the building, got the resources arranged, and found a friendly pastor who was asked to get his church to "sponsor" the new congregation. Because he was a friend, he got the nominal approval of his church. But, before long, many of the churches couldn't remember where "their" mission units were.

In all of these cases, the churches lost the spiritual blessing of involvement and really being part of the missions outreach effort. Further, the mission station lost the spiritual and physical strength of having an involved sponsoring church.

If I were privileged to return to the pastorate in the future and wanted to launch some mission outreach project, I would first make a plan of church preparation. It is doubtful that any pastor ought to take for granted that his church is mission-minded and prepared for mission involvement. A plan of preparation would be a blessing for all involved.

The pastor does a great service to a church by preparing it for missions involvement. Preparing a church for a certain missions task helps educate it for other mission involvements. It is certain that a church which has only token involvement in missions will need much preparation before it undertakes a specific missions task.

Like many of the things of the Christian life, mission mindedness is a learned grace.

In the ideal situation, where a good church missions committee has been selected and trained, the pastor and the committee should meet together for a planning session or a series of planning meetings to develop strategy for preparation of the church for the project of planting mission congregations. Every church needs motivating, educating, and training in order to be prepared for the church planting task. Degrees of need, of course, vary from church to church.

Prepare the Church Through Preaching

The pastor can carefully plan his preaching so it communicates to the church membership an understanding of the real mission of the church. Christ said: "As my Father hath sent me, even so send I you" (John 20:21). As Christ spent himself in the work of redemption, so the church must be willing and ready to spend itself in planned, intelligent, Spirit-led ministry. The church's ministry is a continuation of Christ's ministry, energized by his Spirit.

As the pastor prepares a church for mission outreach, he must build on the mission, ministry, and purpose of Christ himself. The mission of Jesus is quite explicit in the Gospels. A scanning of the Scriptures shows such expressions as:

—He came "to seek and to save that which was lost" (Luke 19:10).

—"He . . . departed to teach and to preach in their cities" (Matt. 11:1).

—He came "to call . . . sinners to repentance" (Matt. 9:13).

—He "came not to be ministered unto, but to minister" (Matt. 20:28).

—"I am come that they might have life" (John 10:10),

Christ declared that the mission of the church is the same as his mission. In John 20:21, he declares: "As my father hath sent me, even so send I you."

In preaching, the pastor needs to magnify the priesthood of the believer—which expresses both the right and the responsibility of every Christian to be involved in the propagation of the gospel. "We are his witnesses" (Acts 5:32) needs to weigh heavily on the heart of every believer until it is no longer a burden but a joyous privilege that is actualized in the lives of the church members.

The pastor, in preaching, needs to emphasize that all believers are ministers of the gospel and that they need to be busy ministering to people in his name. Week-long revival services—or four-day revivals which run Sunday through Wednesday—might be held focusing not on the unchurched but on church members and their commitment to the mission of the church. Revival, by its definition, means to revive the people of God. Revival occurs inside the church, and evangelism takes place outside.

Churches often schedule evangelistic crusades, import a gifted pulpiteer and music director, and then fail to reach many unchurched people. A common response when pastors are asked how such a revival went is, "We didn't have many additions, but we had a great church revival." How much better it would be to plan a church crusade beamed at the church membership, with messages directed to the spiritual needs of the church members. Such a crusade would be good preparation for a church considering the starting of a new mission congregation.

Prepare the Church Through Prayer

One of the basic foundations of church planting is that the Holy Spirit is basic to the whole operation.

Prayer should precede, follow, and intertwine completely through the whole effort. In preparation we must pray much about the project. Special prayer needs to be offered in public services and in prayer groups. Members need to be exhorted to place church extension on their prayer lists. Specific concerns about the project need to be mentioned for prayer. Mission organizations of the church need to focus their praying on the project.

It cannot be emphasized too strongly that prayer is a crucial and indispensable element in church planting. Church planting is a spiritual operation. The church is prepared and the way for the mission is made straight by the prayers of God's people.

Prepare the Church Through Teaching

The missions organizations of the church need to be involved in teaching basic concepts of missions, including mission theology, mission philosophy, and mission history as they relate to church planting. An expansion of the same areas mentioned for the pastor's preaching may be done in the organizations and in other groups within the church.

Special studies may be organized around church planting materials and books which are available from denominational missions organizations.

As the church is taught about missions, the needs of the mission community should be communicated to the church. Communication may be through visuals such as slides or home movies. Testimonies from individuals who have visited the area and studied the situation, or from people in the area who want a new mission may be shared. Needs of the mission community should be inserted in the church bulletin, put on bulletin boards, and displayed in other areas of the church.

One excellent way of teaching the church about mission needs is to take tours of the community where the new church is projected, so members can experience it firsthand.

Prepare the Church Through Training

The initial training, as discussed before, is for the church missions committee. Materials used by the committee may be shared with other church organizational leaders for use in training sessions. Members of the church missions committee are good resource persons to the training leaders in this process.

Training of persons to participate in community surveys is a very early part of the training process. Survey details will be discussed in chapter 7.

Workers also need to be trained for community cultivation. The specifics of community cultivation will be discussed in chapter 7, with many kinds of activities possible. Many of these activities require training, and the church needs to provide it.

Church members may be trained in:

Neighborhood recreation programs.—The use of church recreation clinics to train volunteers who will lead neighborhood recreation programs in the mission community will increase the effectiveness of the cultivation. Training, however, is necessary.

Lay witness schools.—Lay witness teams can be effectively used in cultivation of a new mission community. Fine materials are available to provide training for the individuals and the teams.

Mission-action projects.—Workers in the mission community doing ministry in Jesus' name meet human needs and can build bridges into the new community. Mission-action workshops for such workers in both the doing of the ministry and in the taking of mission-action surveys to determine the needs are very helpful.

Multitudes of community cultivation workers can be used in preparing the field. These three types of methods are only illustrations of the kinds of preparatory training often needed.

The church also should provide training for those persons who will work in fellowship groups. In following chapters, use of home fellowships, home-fellowship missions, home-Bible fellowships, and home-Bible classes will be discussed in detail. However, the church should be aware that leaders for this work need to be trained, as do persons who will work with them in a supportive way. Training could focus on how to begin such a group, how to lead it, how to build attendance, and how to make the group effective.

Much later in the process of planting a new church, volunteers who will lead in the new mission chapel will need to be trained for their task. Hopefully, visitation and home fellowship services in the mission community will have discovered some workers for the new mission. However, many of these need training in the how-to of their task. Potential Sunday School teachers and workers in the mission group could profit by the expertise and training of the mother church. Workers in many other areas of the new mission similarly need training.

The church must be responsible for training lay pastoral leadership. Planting a new church usually implies finding a pastor for the new congregation. In the early stages, while the work is small and financial needs are great, excellent lay preacher leadership often is found in the sponsoring church. A church with an aggressive church extension program may have several mission congregations served by lay preachers. If so, seminary extension training programs may be set up to provide leadership training for these men. Denominational organizations will have information on the resources for such a program. Often, several churches in a region share in such a program of training.

Prepare the Church Through Involvement

The preparation of a church is not a rigid step-by-step process. It flows from action to action, with much overlapping. So it is with the idea of involvement. Through all the stages of preparation, involvement of members of the church in study, in survey, in witness, in discussion, in touring serves to further prepare the church each step of the way.

Prepare the Church Through Commitment

Perhaps this statement sounds ridiculous to some. However, if the church has been prepared through a series of sermons related to missions outreach; if the teaching programs of the church have been communicating needs, concepts, information, motivation; if a continuing emphasis has been given to prayer; if the training of some workers has been done, then a high degree of motivation should become apparent. Commitment is the next logical step.

Opportunities for commitment should be given in several ways. First, at the worship service, an invitation could be given for those who will volunteer to serve in some capacity in the mission project. Other public commitments to pray for the project would be meaningful.

However, the commitment of commitments is in the church business meeting when the congregation officially votes that they will sponsor the planting of a new church in the specific community. The vote should not be taken until much preparation has been made for the step. Earlier votes might have authorized "exploration" or "investigation" or "preliminary studies," all of which fit into a *Plan of Preparation* for the sponsoring church.

The business meeting should be well publicized and members encouraged to attend.

The moment in which a church formally votes to sponsor the starting of a new church ought to be a high and holy moment. Prayer should be offered before the vote. After the vote is taken, the singing of a song of praise would be appropriate. The time should be spiritually enhanced.

Starting a new mission is an eventful step in the life of any church.

7. Cultivate the Field (Step Four)

Rufus Nolan was a young pastor, called to a small mountain church in Coalfield. He was likable and very friendly.

Coalfield was a weak church which needed denominational assistance to provide support for their pastor. Because of a long history of previous assistance, denominational leaders felt the only way aid could be given to the old mission situation was to base it on the church's willingness to allow their pastor to spend half his time in developing a new mission congregation in the resort community of Deep Lake, twenty-three miles away. The church agreed, the position description was prepared, and Nolan began his work.

Immediately after arriving on the field, he started spending two days each week in Deep Lake, just visiting and making friends. The small town had many antique shops, and he spent a lot of time in them, visiting with the dealers and talking about antiques. The community was a resort area and had several fine restaurants. He spent time in the restaurants, drinking coffee and fellowshipping with management and customers. Soon, he was on a first name basis with many of them.

Nolan—known to everybody as Rufus—was identified by most of the people in town at "the pastor who's going to start a new church." In one instance, a businessman's mother died, and Rufus was asked to conduct the funeral. Frequently, his new friends would share the name of a prospect. He'd jot it down and pay a visit.

After seven months of such visiting and fellowshipping, Rufus had his first "home fellowship" meeting. Twenty people came. More than $5,000 was pledged that night for a building fund.

The home fellowship continued for several months, meeting each Thursday night. A church of another denomination sought out

Nolan and invited the group to use the church building on Sunday morning at an alternate hour. It was the result of community cultivation.

National missions assistance helped purchase a building site, since Deep Lake is a resort community in a county that is 85 percent unchurched. A team of fourteen college students and an adult sponsor were enlisted to construct the building during the summer months.

The young pastor, with almost no resources, went out one day to try to find a place for his team of students to live for the summer. Housing was at a premium in the resort area during the summer. However, across the street from the church site, Nolan found a large, rambling, vacant house, just right for the team. He checked and found it belonged to one of the businessmen with whom he had become friends. Checking further, he found it normally rented for $400 per month during the summer. The friendship prevailed, and the businessman insisted on providing the house rent free. It was the result of community cultivation.

One day another businessman stopped Nolan on the street and said, "You know, you're going to need a stove and refrigerator for those college students. I have bought them and put them in the house. When you get the church built, put them in the kitchen." It was the result of community cultivation.

Another day, as he continued to prepare for the summer construction project, the manager of the finest restaurant in town called. "That is such a fine project that I'd like to give those college students and their sponsors their Sunday dinner free every Sunday during the summer." It was again the result of community cultivation.

The students arrived and built a lovely chapel and educational building.

While they were working, the students found time to make friends in the community. In the summer evenings, teams of musical troubadours wandered around, singing ballads and gospel songs. Often, they did chalk talks and drama. They had puppet shows. On occasion, they formed a choir and gave simple gospel concerts. All of this was still community cultivation.

Toward the end of the summer, dedication Sunday arrived. In the small town of 1,000 nearly 500 people tried to get into the *small chapel designed for 125 people. The town had fallen in love with the students and with the young minister, simply because they took time to make friends.*

The basic principle of community cultivation is simply to identify two things: community needs and community interests. Cultivative activities may then be beamed to either a need or an interest, and the worker may anticipate good response.

Apart from selecting the right community in which to plant a new church, perhaps the single most important element in a right beginning is community cultivation. A carefully designed plan of community cultivation should be developed by the church missions committee. It should have room to add other elements that emerge as the workers become more familiar with the community. It should be flexible enough to eliminate, change, or redirect any activity as the situation requires.

An Example: Dave Logan was conducting a mission Vacation Bible School to cultivate a neighborhood in a large midwestern city. No one came the first day. Dave looked the situation over and found that he was in a heavily non-Christian, non-Protestant, largely unchurched community. The very name "Vacation Bible School" created problems.

He quickly renamed the activities "Neighborhood Recreation Program," added more recreation, reduced the Bible content a little, and had hundreds of kids.

Through the children, Logan found names and addresses of parents who were prospects for a new church effort.

Elements of the Community Cultivation Plan

The sponsoring church should formulate a carefully devised plan to cultivate the community where the new mission will be located. It should be flexible, but it also should be as well organized as possible, providing a guide for the operation.

Some General Principles

The needs and interests of the community should be investigated and should determine the types of cultivation events, ministries, and activities.

Church planters also should remember that community problems are opportunities. One pastor has suggested that churches "utilize your problematic opportunities." For example, if baby-sitters are scarce in the area, a baby-sitting ministry or a "drop-off" center should be devised to help open doors.

Many times churches get anxious and jump too quickly into having worship services. An adequate period of cultivation should precede any effort to have services, either in homes or in a public place. The length of time will vary from community to community, so the workers will have to sense when the time is right to move into more solid work. The Holy Spirit will guide the worker in making this determination.

The church or worker also should remember what he's there for. A redemptive note must be maintaned in all cultivative activities. Many examples could be shared of situations where all sorts of friendly community contacts were made, but no one came to know Christ. The reason was that no mention was made of the fact that Jesus Christ loves sinners, came to save sinners, and that he wants to save every person. Without the redemptive note, a wonderful social-action program can be developed, but that's not a church.

All cultivative work should be fortified by using Bible-study groups. These groups will be discussed in detail in chapter 8, but Bible-study groups are where cultivation starts to merge into the birth of the church. Friends are made in cultivation; Christians are made in Bible-study groups. It is imperative that these things go hand in hand, to give meaning to all the labor involved in cultivating the field.

Identifying the Unchurched

Cultivation should be aimed at identifying the unchurched. There are a number of methods to accomplish this, such as surveying, cultivative events, and community involvement.

A survey should be made of the entire area where the new church is proposed in order to determine the number of prospects and, more importantly, to determine exactly *who* is a prospect by name, address, age, sex, and religious background.

Occasionally, churches of several denominations are willing to work together for a cooperative survey. It cultivates community goodwill, eliminates fear of proselyting, and provides a lot more workers.

When such a cooperative survey is made, prospects may be shared several ways. One method is to divide the cards by church preference. Another is to enlist volunteer typists from participating churches who would type a complete list of the prospects, placing the data in columns opposite the name. Thus, all participating churches have a listing of all prospects.

In preparing for the survey, church leaders should determine the method of taking the survey. Most common methods are canvassing door-to-door and telephoning.

In door-to-door surveys, the entire community should be mapped clearly so that no worker overlaps and so no house is overlooked. Supplies usually consist of family survey cards which contain spaces for several members of the family on each card. The cards should be kept in a 5" by 7" envelope, on which the worker maps the blocks he or she surveys.

Survey workers should be instructed to complete every blank on the cards, with special attention given to the address. (Samples of the card and envelope are in Appendices C and D.)

The workers should also be instructed not to get into extended discussions with the residents but to concentrate on getting information with the thought of later vists for discussion or witness.

It is recommended that survey workers approach a house with this general approach:

"Good morning. We are taking a church community survey. Could you spare a moment to complete a card on your family? (Without a pause) Where does your family attend church? Do all of you go there? . . . ."

If the family attends church as a unit, time is conserved by thanking the person and moving on. If the response is otherwise, complete the card. Workers should not get involved in debate, and they should always be polite.

If a telephone survey is preferred, the same cards can be used, but a street directory is needed so calls can be guided to a specific neighborhood. If the entire community is being surveyed, the regular telephone book can be used. Similar instructions apply in completing the cards and in making the approach. Always stress that the worker should never get into extended conversations, or the survey would never be completed.

After the method of survey has been determined, a date must be set when the survey will be taken and volunteers enlisted. Many surveys have been successful on Saturday because more volunteers are available and more people seem to be at home. A sizable neighborhood can be surveyed in person or by phone in one day if the workers closely follow the instuctions.

Some workers have attempted to prepare the way for the survey by a special mailing to all homes with a form that can be prepared and given to the survey taker. Others have tried newspaper advertising, and still others have distributed handbills or brochures. Generally, it appears none of these things are of much help.

Whether taking the survey by telephone or door-to-door, the survey worker should note the address or telephone number on a blank card when no one is home, so follow-up workers can complete the blind spots. Workers should be enlisted and dates set to follow up on the "not at homes" promptly so the survey will give a complete picture. Some key prospects might be in the "not at home" file.

After the survey is completed, a first-class prospect file should be developed, using the best forms available in the church supply store. This again provides opportunity for church member involvement, and the cards should be typed so they will be legible to any visitation worker.

Another method of identifying the unchurched is through community events. Historically, mission Vacation Bible Schools have been one of the most commonly used cultivative events. Careful registration of children, including names and addresses of parents and church affiliations, forms a good file for follow up activity. "Parents' Night" at the end of school, when certificates are awarded, also provides a good opportunity for workers to meet parents and to make friends.

Neighborhood recreation programs function much the same way. They can be multiple recreation efforts—using Fun Wagons especially equipped for the effort—or more limited games, like baseball or basketball. Registration lists provide contact with homes. Choir concerts, music festivals, dramatic presentations, and puppet shows also can be used as community events to gain attention, make friends, and open doors.

Probably the most historic cultivative effort in the Protestant tradition is the mission revival meeting. Many churches across America were born out of revival meetings. In certain socioeconomic and cultural groups, and in certain areas, the mission revival is still a valid technique for community cultivation, particularly if it is well done.

Another way to identify the unchurched is through community involvement. By taking part in the life of the community—through activities, organizations, and events—workers can accumulate a list of many key unchurched people in a community. One worker systematically visited and fellowshipped in places of business, tactfully discovering church relationships which he later used in follow-up.

Building Community Relationships

In new areas, where the church is not known, the development of a good image is a logical early step in the cultivaton process. By maintaining a gracious spirit in contact with community leaders and institutions, future doors of opportunity may open.

Church planting workers should make contact with existing churches and church organizations, seeking to meet their leaders. Assurance should be given that the new churches do not desire to proselyte but want only to join hands with existing churches in seeking to reach the unchurched and to give a more adequate ministry to the community.

If there are institutions of higher learning, visits to key administrative personnel may be helpful. Particularly important are visits to directors of campus ministry or professors of religion, if the school has such a department. These contacts may prove helpful in contacting college young people who desire to share in the new fellowship.

Church planters should seek to know the leaders in government and business, as well as professionals in the helping services (welfare, social work, and so forth). Contacts with schools and real estate agents also are helpful in making contacts and building friendships.

Building Personal Relationships

During the community survey, alert workers can identify some of the needs of the community: child care, alcoholism, lonely, old people, single-parent's families, drug addiction, illiteracy, English as a second language, and so on. In order to build personal relationships, church planters should seek to build relationships by developing a ministry to meet some need in the community. Community agencies, schools, government offices, and individuals will provide information on inquiry. Articles in the local newspaper also will provide a clue to the needs of the community.

Asking questions also will help uncover community needs and interests, and conversations with prospects will help the alert church worker determine the desires and problems which he can then work to help meet.

As the worker discovers needs and interests, he should begin to work toward developing ministries to help meet them. One small church discovered an interest in knitting. In a few weeks a dozen ladies were enrolled in a knitting class, and many warm personal relationships were established.

Adult ministries have included such things as home discussion groups on drug and narcotic problems, dieting, citizenship classes, alcoholism. All of these programs bring people together around a common need, and many churches have had effective and helpful programs which have built bridges to the community because of an identified need and an effort on the part of the church to meet that need.

Visitation in Homes and Businesses

After contacts have been made and lists of prospects have been prepared, visitation is the logical culmination of all the cultivative activities.

In most churches, visitation is the most poorly organized part of the church program. Workers are scarce and often untrained. Results are few and frustrations are many. In a mission situation where a new church is being planted, it is imperative that visitation be well organized and smoothly functioning.

Church planting visitation also must be unapologetically evangelistic in its thrust. New churches are formed largely with new converts or reclaimed Christians who have been inactive. If a person is timid about sharing his faith with an evangelistic purpose, he will not be an effective visitor in church planting.

A program simply will not and cannot succeed without an updated and accurate list of prospects. It is the very life blood of any visitation program.

Ideally, visitors in a church planting cultivation project need a time for sharing with each other, reporting on visits, making prayer requests, and spending time praying together about successes and failures.

A good visitation program also will offer workers a variety of options. A stated night might be good for some persons, while a daytime assignment is good for others. Some visitors like to take cards and make visits at their own convenience, returning the cards within a week. Also, visitation by appointment is a good method when cultivating a new community. People appreciate not having their meals interrupted or their favorite television program disrupted. Such a visit is often more effective because the person being visited is calmer, more relaxed, and receptive to a meaningful discussion.

Demonstrating Love and Concern for People

The methods of community cultivation are not ends in themselves; they are a means to help discover people who need the love and concern of God's people. We, as God's people, are to show God's love to all people. That's what community cultivation and church planting are all about: showing people that God loves them, and that they need Jesus Christ in their lives.

A word of caution: the love we show must be genuine; the care must come from our hearts. The ministries begun in church planting operations—ministries to senior citizens, Mothers-Day-Out projects, Citizenship classes—demonstrate that the Christian workers seeking to plant a new church love people, are concerned about people and are entering the community to help meet the real needs of people.

Church-planting workers need to relate to community activities that are wholesome and worthwhile, so that the proposed new church does not appear to be a parasite on the community and so that the intention of the church is never brought into question. The new church should emerge on the scene showing an interest in the total welfare of the community.

Church-planting workers need to maintain a wholesome, cooperative spirit with existing churches from the very beginning. No church planter gains any ground when he appears to say, "We've come to this community to show all you folks how to have a real, genuine church," implying that the existing churches are not real and genuine. No church planter should have a chip-on-his-shoulder attitude toward existing churches, nor speak critically of them.

He must maintain a gracious spirit to all people.

The church planter who shows Christian graciousness toward all and who sounds a positive note in the community will find a more ready response to his endeavor.

8. The Mission Fellowship (Step Five)

La Linda Church, in the growing area along the Southern border of the United States, was challenged by Pastor Herman Rohrer to establish a mission.

Under the leadership of the pastor and the church missions committee, data was gathered on the city. Since there were thirty-two churches of the denomination in the city, the missions committee looked to the Southwestern section which was experiencing a building boom and increasing population.

Neighborhoods were charted and an intensive program of cultivation was started. Backyard Bible clubs reached hundreds of children and through them a detailed prospect list was prepared. Recreation—using a Fun Wagon—reached many other children, primarily young teenagers. Choir concerts were held in a new shopping mall on Saturday afternoons and evenings, and the young people of the church received permission from the mall management to use a small area for a baby-sitting service for mothers who wished to shop in the large facility.

Evangelistic visitation was coupled with the cultivative activity.

Finally, after six months, six members of the church who lived in the growing area were asked to open their homes for mission fellowships. When they agreed, the residents were provided extensive training, and mission fellowships were started. One met in Fred Franco's home. Big game trophies dotted the walls of the huge den. Another fellowship met each Thursday night in the basement of the William Stone home. Others met in living rooms, family rooms, and one even met in a garage.

The training of the lay leaders continued through the fellowship period, giving them information and resource material for their work.

Some church members pressed to form the fellowships into a mission chapel, but Pastor Rohrer advised moving slowly. "They must have time to develop."

The fellowships met for two years, occasionally coming together for a big Sunday afternoon rally in the auditorium of the shopping mall. Two of the fellowships dwindled away and died, but four remained and continued to reach out.

After two years and after unit meetings and a group meeting, the time had come to start a mission chapel. A steering committee was formed, and the group, meeting with the pastor and the La Linda Church missions committee, obtained the auditorium of a school and launched a full program of Sunday School, Christian training, worship services, and Bible study.

After careful planning, Southwest chapel was formed with a strong nucleus of forty families—more than 100 persons.

After a period of intense community cultivation where friends have been made, spiritual needs identified, and ministries begun, it is time to begin drawing the people together, giving the seeds which have been planted an opportunity to grow. In most cases, the most effective way to do this is through home fellowships. These fellowships become an embryo congregation which evolves from the earlier contacts.

These small fellowship groups go by many names across the nation. Some are called "Home Fellowship Missions," some are called "Fellowship Bible Classes" and others are referred to as "Bible Study Fellowships." Still others are called home or neighborhood Bible classes. Many groups have renewal as their purpose. Still others are formed for in-depth Bible study, ministry, local church expansion, fellowship.

For the purposes of this book, we shall refer to the small group as a mission fellowship and note its purpose is to be an embryonic form of a new church being born. It's aim is to reach the unchurched and inactive Christians.

John H. Allen, in "Missions Fellowships," says: "What makes mission fellowships such an effective tool in . . . church extension? It starts from a zero base. No building, budget or Madison Avenue type public relations is necessary to gather a nucleus—just one dedicated man or woman. One person with an open heart, an open Bible and an open living room is sufficient to begin. No messianic announcement is made by skywriting at noonday over the public market places of the city, just a friendly, nonthreatening invitation by a neighbor to come over for coffee and Christian fellowship."

Why a Mission Fellowship Period Is Needed

The small group exists to evangelize new converts and inactive Christians and to help them develop into effective, serving Christians who can be a nucleus of workers in a new church. The process takes time; a suitable period is needed to allow the nucleus to develop into a fellowship of mature believers.

Allen outlines five reasons why such a fellowship period is important:

First, the new work needs time to solidify its base. Not everyone comes into the group with the same dedication, experience, and concepts. Time is needed to solidify the purpose and commitment of the group.

Second, a new work needs time to develop Christian fellowship. The love level and trust level (they are the same) of a group must be developed as a base for all future relationships. People do not trust or love those whom they do not know. A small, informal group meeting in homes encourages learning more than does the typical chapel model of "preaching and departing."

Third, the new work needs time to broaden its base. The fellowship period provides the nucleus time to build a financial base. Practically no funds are needed at this stage, so a wise leader will hold mission and building funds for future use. A sound financial policy gives credibility to the new work without and builds pride within.

Fourth, a new work needs time to discover its leaders. Troubled people often seek out new work, not for what they can give, but for what they can get to meet their own needs. True leaders will emerge in time, but the ones who become the leaders will not always be the ones who initially emerge or "announce" their position. Group experience brings out the best and worst in potential leaders. Time should be allowed for these leaders to emerge or the results will be tragic. Persons with the most intense desire to lead are not always the ones who should be given that responsibility.

Fifth, a new work needs time to train and develop its leaders. A solid base of Christian discipleship and churchmanship is needed before launching into the time-consuming tasks of organizational and administrative training necessary to maintain a new church program. Initially, attention should be devoted to soul-winning, stewardship, prayer life, and the general development of a sound spiritual life. This period also should feature grounding in the biblically based doctrines of the church. This teaching and training prepares the leaders for an effective ministry to the community when the chapel or mission is formally organized.

If a solid foundation is laid, the cost counted, and leadership tested, the fallout from the mission will be slight.

Various Styles of Mission Fellowships

The mission fellowship with a missionary thrust—one designed to give birth to a new church congregation—may appear in many forms and kinds.

One common group is the Bible-study group, which has as its purpose the reaching, discipling, and developing of new converts. Another is the contact group, which is an action-oriented set of Christians making contact with non-Christians on the fringe area of the church through action or encounter events, such as a choir concert. Another group might be task oriented; a specialized force to witness to a particular segment of society, such as the handicapped, deaf, blind, illiterate, singles, or divorced persons.

Another type of group is the worship group, which gathers for a worship experience. What has been historically called a "preaching point" may well be a mission fellowship which features singing of hymns, prayers, and a sermon or Bible lesson.

Another group is the Christian-forum group, which discusses topics of community interest, gaining biblical insights and awakening spiritual interests.

How to Establish a Mission Fellowship

Before a mission fellowship is established, the church missions committee should have been active, identifying areas of need, selecting target communities, and leading in intensive community cultivation.

The meeting place can be almost anywhere, but the home is the most satisfactory place in most cases. The living room, den, family room, dining room, or basement are good places, depending on the size of the group. Even a garage or patio can be used, depending on the climate of the area.

Other sites might be hotel or motel conference rooms, civic halls, community rooms of banks or apartment complexes, mobile chapels, schools, churches of other denominations, store buildings, or restaurants. One very successful fellowship was a breakfast group in a restaurant. By special arrangement, prior to opening the restaurant to the general public, breakfast was served to about forty men in a Bible-fellowship study group.

In choosing a place—particularly a home—care should be taken to make sure there is not some community distaste for the home owner. For example, community response would not be too high if the meeting place was in the home of the "community grouch" who complained about everyone's children walking on his lawn.

Many persons fear that a mission fellowship can become a problem group. However, if proper church preparation has been made, the sponsoring church will be guiding the fellowship through the church missions committee. If the sponsoring church provides adequate training, leadership, and guidance, there is very little difference between Room 222 of the Education Building and 222 Walnut Street. The key is to elect and train the persons who will lead the fellowship group and to provide continued support.

If the mission fellowship is to be a Bible-study group, training in good Bible-teaching methods is essential. Choice of good curriculum material also is crucial. A nondescript, emerging group should not be left to their own whims and fancies as to the choice of Bible-study material. It would then become a case of shared ignorance or the blind leading the blind. New and inactive Christians do not possess the spiritual maturity to make the best choices in these beginning days and often can be enticed down some side road if not carefully led.

If the mission fellowship is to feature a worship service, the leader may be some lay person who has taught adult Bible classes for many years and is experienced in thinking on his feet. If the church plans an extensive outreach program using lay pastors, a comprehensive training program which offers study on pastoral ministries, management, leadership, and sermon preparation is desirable. Such courses are often available in extension or correspondence courses. The church should provide the best material available.

Many persons who feel uncomfortable in a study situation and/or cannot attend Sunday worship, enjoy the worship service type of fellowship best. Because the fellowship meets in homes, musical instruments often will not be available. Use of a guitar or taped accompaniment may be considered, but leaders also likely will wish to use familiar hymns and gospel songs. They may design a bulletin for the fellowship with the order of worship on the front, words of the songs on the inside pages and the responsive reading on the back.

Taking an offering depends on the situation. If taken, it should be submitted to the treasurer of the sponsoring church. If the group meets regularly and takes offerings frequently, reports should be made on how the funds are being used.

Also, in the worship type fellowship, the leader should take care not to abuse the time. The service should be brief; services lasting more than an hour interfere with other obligations, work schedules, and children who have to attend school the next day.

If the mission fellowship is to be a Christian forum or discussion group, the leader should be elected by the church and provided good orientation. If the discussion is on some community issue, the leader should recruit resource persons to aid the study.

The Christian forum may be started of unchurched persons or inactive Christians. As their spiritual lives are made active through conversion or renewal, the group may wish to change to a worship group.

Christian forum groups also are needed to train new converts or renewed Christians, grounding them in Christian doctrine, stewardship, church polity, and other matters as they move toward becoming a new congregation.

Dealing with Problems

A mission fellowship involved in Bible study often attracts a "crank" or troublesome person who comes to disrupt or disturb. Such persons need to be dealt with firmly. A private visit to the person may be necessary. Occasionally, for the sake of the whole group and the needs of the community, the leader may have to ask such a person not to attend.

An Example: Joe Falls was a mess. He retired and meddled in everything in the community. He didn't mean ill, he just irritated everyone and was very obnoxious. When members of Pine Street Church started a Bible fellowship in his neighborhood, Joe was one of the first ones to sign up. Every session became a long discourse by Joe on some item he found interesting. One time it was the Jehovah's Witnesses, another time world religions. Often he just rambled along about anything. When new people came to the fellowship, they were turned off by Joe. After several months of suffering through Joe's disruptions, lay-pastor Jim Willis visited Joe's home to discuss the problems. When Joe understood what problems he was causing, he learned to keep his mouth shut. By dealing with Joe, Willis was able to improve the study and increase the fellowship's outreach.

In another situation, four attempts were made to start a fellowship. They were disrupted each time by a troublesome woman. Finally, the fifth time, the leader visited her home and informed her that the group respectfully asked her not to attend their meetings. That time the fellowship began and a thriving church was started from the nucleus.

Some lay persons have been hesitant to lead a mission fellowship for fear someone would ask a hard question they could not answer. The fellowship leader should unashamedly indicate to the group that he does not have all the answers. He should tell them any question he cannot answer will be recorded and researched during the week. He may refer to a good commentary or talk with the pastor. The sponsoring church's library should provide a set of good commentaries for the fellowship leaders' use in preparation and teaching.

Attendance problems often plague a group. The leaders should be assisted by other workers in visitation, writing letters, making phone calls, distributing brochures, and promoting attendance in other ways. Involvement by group members in promoting attendance and in making contacts with the unchurched or inactive can be very meaningful.

Lagging attendance can indicate problems in several areas: meeting time, meeting place, style of leadership, and content of the discussion.

The effective leader should study attendance and move to correct problems when they occur. He should not let them escalate into major obstacles. Low attendance may be the result of an awkard time, one which unnecessarily conflicts with other activities. For instance, in towns where high school sports are popular, Friday night would be a poor choice for a fellowship, as it generally conflicts with football, basketball, and other athletic events.

Low attendance also may indicate problems with the meeting place. For instance, an unairconditioned home in warm weather may cause members to be uncomfortable and quit coming.

The teacher's style of teaching or leadership also may cause lagging attendance. Some fellowship leaders have been heard to say: "Boy, we had a great meeting at our Bible-study group. We talked and talked for three hours and still didn't want to go home." Actually, that might mean the leader was having a great time while the people were wishing he would hush and adjourn. Leaders who abuse the time of the members often face empty rooms.

Another factor in poor attendance may be the content of the discussion: people are not interested by the topic of the study. After tactful checking, the leader may wish to change the curriculum.

Another problem in leading mission fellowships is knowing when to make changes. Possible changes confronting the fellowship are:

* When to divide the group into two or more;
* When to change the nature of the fellowship group from Bible study to worship or to forum;
* When to change the curriculum.

Many groups want to move too quickly into a Sunday-morning worship. It is hoped that when the group becomes too large for a home, it will divide into two or more and wait until strength is sufficient for formation into a chapel. Often separating into several groups will diversify the base of the chapel group, reaching new communities and probing new neighborhoods. Hopefully, the group will remain a mission fellowship until at least four groups are meeting in different parts of the community.

The groups may be divided according to interests. One may be formed of new converts, another of reclaimed Christians, and still another of persons studying Christian doctrine. Such groups could provide strong leadership training for those who will participate in the Sunday School or other organizations of the new congregation, when it is formed.

The unity of the fellowship group—even when divided into a number of segments—could be preserved by Sunday afternoon rallies, bringing all units together at a central place. It helps retain the bond of love and trust which has been formed.

Children and Youth During the Fellowship Period

Children's Bible clubs may be formed in the neighborhoods, as after-school meetings in homes on an age-graded basis. A mix of recreation, fellowship, and Bible teaching make this a wholesome learning experience. Children involved in such clubs become door openers to visitation of adults by the adult mission fellowship groups.

Youth groups, patterned much like the adult mission fellowships, can meet at the convenience of the youth of the neighborhood and can be a vital part of the emerging congregation. Use of music, as well as Bible discussion, can make a youth mission fellowship a meaningful experience.

Care should be taken, however, that children and youth are provided spiritual experiences during the meetings of the adult fellowship. Such children's activities, particularly, should never be merely baby-sitting exercises. Programs will differ from group to group, but the effective leader will seek opportunities to make such activities meaningful to children and youth.

One note of caution: Often when parents are reached for Jesus Christ and become involved in church, mission, or fellowship, their children are left behind. Care should be exercised to make sure children and young people are evangelized and taught—in organization and in the home—effectively.

How Long Should a Fellowship Continue?

One of the most frequently asked questions about fellowships is: How long should the group remain in a home fellowship situation before it moves to more formal Sunday worship services?

There is no single answer to the question, but there are guidelines which might be helpful.

First, consider the community served. Is the adult nucleus large enough to staff a beginning Sunday School and worship service? Would there be suitable teachers for each age group and for general officers? Is there sufficient manpower to provide adequate leadership for each of the programs involved in a mission organization?

Second, consider the group itself. Is there a sense of unity and oneness of purpose? The fellowship period tends to develop togetherness much more effectively than does formal church life.

Third, consider maturity. Has there been a study of the basics of Christian doctrine, church polity, teaching methods, spiritual life, stewardship, prayer?

Fourth, consider finances. Has a sufficient financial base emerged? Do the people understand stewardship and their responsibility to support the work?

Fifth, consider commitment. Have the members of the fellowship group committed themselves to beginning a new church?

Reviewing these guidelines, as well as the basic reasons why the fellowship was begun, will be helpful in determining if the time is right to move from a home fellowship into a more formal worship service.

Premature beginning may be disastrous; it may result in loss of the group and of the ultimate congregation. Readiness is as important to a new church as it is to a child's development.

9. The Mission Chapel (Step Six)

Hiram Hartford looked closely at the group of seven families who were participating in the home Bible fellowship at his residence. For eight months they had been meeting regularly and faithfully each Thursday night.

Hartford was the leader of the small group. They were "his" people. He had visited in each home personally and was involved closely with them.

The outreach had begun as an extension of Trinity Church, and Hiram worked closely with the church missions committee in cultivative events and preparation for the fellowship.

Now, after seven months, the small unit had become church for Hiram Hartford. His attendance at Trinity lagged, and his contact with the church missions committee lessened as he threw all his efforts and interests into the small Thursday night fellowship.

As he looked at his small "congregation," Hiram decided it was time to begin a mission chapel, complete with Sunday School, worship services, and a regular Wednesday night Bible study.

He talked with the church missions committee. Members were somewhat reluctant, concerned about whether there were sufficient resources, leadership, and commitment to the project. But Hiram was a forceful personality and he believed very strongly in what he was about to do. His view prevailed as members acquiesced.

With sponsorship funds, Hiram found an auditorium at the American Legion hall and announced services. He bought an ad in the community paper and put posters in supermarkets and discount stores around the area.

Hiram, his wife Betty, and their two small children appeared bright and early that Sunday morning. Their faces were eager and they wore their best Sunday-go-to meeting clothes.

*When 10:00 A.M. came, Hiram and his family were in the echoing
hall alone. No one else came. The time ticked by. Eleven o'clock
rolled past with no one else there. Hiram was alone.*

*Hiram was crushed. He had been ready, but the seven young
couples in the Thursday night fellowship weren't. Hiram mis-
judged and started services prematurely.*

Care should be exercised in beginning Sunday chapel services.
Premature services often cause more problems than they solve.
Leaders of home fellowship missions should carefully judge their
groups and engage in a meticulous study before beginning services.

There are many dangers involved in beginning chapel services
prematurely. The members may be spiritually immature, leadership
may be limited, finances and resources may be inadequate, and
the participants may be committed to the units but not to Sunday
services.

When beginning services, the group needs to be certain pastoral
and lay leadership is sufficient for the new congregation. Needs and
responsibilities are heavier in a congregation and with rent, utilities,
outreach, programs, needs are intensified.

If a fellowship group begins services prematurely, it may be too
weak to continue ministering to its own members or to attract new
members. Often a weak mission is less attractive to new members
than is a strong fellowship unit.

Another danger which many people often overlook is the danger
of distortion. When a first effort fails, a second start is much more
difficult. The chapel's reputation is questioned. It is easier to create
a good impression the first time than it is to correct a distortion.

Church planters should consider several questions before beginning a chapel.

First, is leadership adequate? Lay and pastoral leadership is
needed to staff an entire program. If there is insufficient leadership,
the chapel will not function effectively. If there is lack of financial
and spiritual leadership, the mission may be ineffective.

Second, does the community need another church? The initial
decision to begin a new work in the community was made as the
fellowships started. However, after operating mission fellowships
in a community over a period of time, the church missions committee and fellowship leadership should weigh carefully the need for

a church in the community. As the fellowship has operated, leadership should have received new insights into the community. Occasionally, it is found that a mission fellowship in a home is an adequate witness for that community. No church is needed.

Third, is the membership mature? If members are not sufficiently mature in their Christian life, fellowship problems may emerge. Along with their maturity also comes the question of their commitment. Are they committed to beginning a mission chapel?

Fourth, is the group growing? If the units are not experiencing numerical as well as spiritual growth there is a question about its expansion as a chapel.

Steps Toward Becoming a Mission Chapel

As the fellowship units—and the sponsoring church's missions committee—plan toward mission chapel status, a careful and detailed plan of action should be devised.

First, the fellowship should work closely with the sponsoring church through the church missions committee. It should request permission from the mother church to become a mission chapel. Details of the relationship should be clearly understood, and the church missions committee should formalize their understandings.

All aspects of the relationship should be clearly understood. Many details must be arranged and bylaws should be written to govern relationships and responsibilities between the sponsoring church and the chapel.

Bylaws should include:

• The method of reception of members by the chapel, including those who come by letter, baptism, or statement;

• The handling of mission finances and budget should be clarified. The mission should have some involvement in formulating and developing the budget. Members of the chapel should be kept informed on all receipts and expenditures. The sponsoring church should establish a mission account, depositing and drawing funds from and for the mission in that account.

• The business operation of the mission should be explained in the bylaws. Normally, mission congregations do not have business meetings but rather recommendation services in which they make recommendations to the sponsoring church for approval. Representatives from the mission should attend meetings of the church missions committee and of the church conference of the sponsoring church.

• The method and frequency of reports from the mission chapel to the sponsor should be defined. Normally, missions congregations report their Sunday statistics each Monday and then submit a comprehensive monthly report to the church missions committee for transmission to the church business meeting.

• The procedure for selecting a worship leader or pastor of the mission should be clearly outlined in the bylaws. Normally, the church missions committee, with chapel representation, is the pulpit committee for the mission congregation in considering prospective mission pastors. When a prospective pastor is brought for consideration, he usually preaches at the mission Sunday morning and at the sponsoring church Sunday night. When the mission congregation makes its recommendation, it is forwarded to the church for action.

• The process or choosing of chapel officers and teachers should be set forth in the mission bylaws.

• The selection and responsibilities of chapel representatives to the church missions committee should be indicated in the bylaws.

• Authorization for chapel observance of baptism and the Lord's Supper should be included in the bylaws.

In addition to the bylaws, other important matters of sponsor-chapel relationships should be determined before the chapel begins holding services. These include:

• The amount of program the chapel will undertake in the initial stages and at what point other elements will be added. Provision for the chapel to be served by elements of the sponsoring church's program should be considered when proximity makes it possible.

• The amount of support the sponsor will provide, including money, lay membership, leadership, and church staff. Often the minister of education and minister of music of the sponsoring church can assist the chapel by working with mission leadership to provide educational and music programs.

Preparing to Begin

As details of relationships are being worked out, the church missions committee and fellowship leadership should begin an intensive program of preparation for the beginning of the chapel.

The community should be thoroughly cultivated as preparations for the new chapel get underway. Methods of cultivation were extensively discussed in chapter 7, and new round of these cultivative activities should be started. A new schedule of choir concerts, backyard-Bible clubs, ministries, and evangelistic visitation programs should immediately precede the formal Sunday services.

The members of the fellowship units also should be prepared for the start of services. Leadership should make sure those who have been attending the units are emotionally and spiritually ready for the transition to chapel services. The members need to be committed firmly to involvement in the chapel. Many people are lost in this type of transition when commitment is not secured.

Leaders of the fellowship units also must explain to all chapel members their relationship to the sponsoring church and should lead every member to be as completely involved as possible in planning and preparation for the first Sunday.

Leaders should carefully prepare the initial service. This involves choosing a date to start, but it does not end there. Preparation includes selecting the site, the worship leader, and the order of service. It entails making sure adequate literature is on hand, that spaces have been allocated for all Sunday School classes, and that teachers will be present.

Preparation for the inaugural service also involves prayer. Fellowship units, the church missions committee, and the sponsoring church should be called into prayer—real, fervent prayer—for the success and outreach of the venture.

When selecting a date to start, leaders should choose a Sunday as free from all distracting activities as is possible. The inaugural date should not be on a holiday weekend, on Mother's Day, commencement Sunday, or any such conflicting time. By selecting a "free" date, chapel leaders will free the initial service from unnecessary competition.

The meeting site is important. It should be as attractive as possible, convenient, and appropriate to the life-style of the community. It should be adequate in size and creature comforts, such as heating or air conditioning. When inspecting potential sites, workers should take nothing for granted but should use a checklist which has been prepared beforehand, listing what they consider to be essential components.

Those preparing the inaugural service also should be sensitive in selecting the worship leader. The worship leader needs to be enlisted far in advance for the inaugural Sunday and for all succeeding Sundays. Many mission congregations start initially with a lay preacher or with a bi-vocational pastor. Some groups have mission worship at an earlier hour and use the pastor of the sponsoring church as their worship leader. Such an arrangement permits the pastor to be back at the mother church to lead services there. Other options include using the director of missions or a staff member of the regional organization or a staff member of the sponsoring church as pastor of the new congregation.

Publicity is an essential ingredient in starting a new mission. The material should be carefully prepared and as widely distributed as possible. News articles with good photographs are usually welcomed by the local newspaper. Where possible, friendly relationships should have been developed with editors and writers of the newspaper during the community cultivation process. This relationship should not be viewed as a vehicle to get publicity in the paper but as an opportunity to make friends and to reach those persons who work in journalistic fields, whether they are unchurched or inactive. If the relationship is established only to get the publicity in the paper, the Christian likely will be viewed as a manipulator and the effort will turn sour.

An effort also should be made to get good publicity photos, even if it requires hiring a photographer. Fuzzy, out-of-focus, and poorly composed pictures will not be used. Many congregations also may wish to obtain photos of the inaugural service.

Publicity releases should be well done, short, to the point, and accurate. The news media generally will not use windy, "preacherish" articles which are lacking in adequate facts and long on ecclesiastical language.

Publicity—including posters, signs, handouts, brochures, news articles in newspaper, radio, and television—should be well done, if it is to be effective.

Frequently overlooked is public relations. Persons who wish to come to the initial service should readily find the meeting place. Signs should be placed outside and at other strategic locations directing visitors and members of the service. Also, ushers should be placed at key places to give instructions and directions.

A critical ingredient is the way people are treated once they get there. Often the first impression is the only one we get a chance to give. If people are unfavorably impressed by the organization, information, friendliness, and helpfulness, they likely will not come back.

Careful preparation is the key to a successful initial service. Leave nothing to chance; plan, check, and meticulously carry through. Sunday School literature and materials must be ordered well in advance; hymnals need to be obtained in plenty of time for the first service; musical instruments—piano or organ—should be obtained if they are not available in the meeting place. Other equipment—lectern, chairs, classroom dividers, pulpit furniture, portable nursery equipment—also must be on hand on that first Sunday.

Generally the site is used for other activities during the week, and leaders should attempt to secure a storage cabinet for materials, thus easing the pain of transporting everything every Sunday and lessening the chance that some essential item will be forgotten.

Careful planning of every phase of the first Sunday is necessary. But, as a reminder, every person involved needs to be aware that what is happening is not just an organizational exercise; it is a spiritual endeavor, dedicated to God and led by the Holy Spirit. If it is to be a success, every step must be immersed in prayer, and every person must constantly seek the guidance and leadership of the Holy Spirit.

The Program of the Mission Chapel

As the mission chapel begins, it should have a program commensurate with its resources and membership. It should, of course, include Sunday School, worship, training events, and Bible study.

Where possible, the chapel should secure a music leader with capabilities of organizing and directing a small choir. In fact, the choir should sing for the first service if it is practical to do so.

The chapel should include those programs, services, and organizations which are needed in the beginning to serve the congregation and to attract new members and converts.

As new programs are added, leadership should choose meeting times carefully, attempting to schedule them at times which do not compete with other activities, either in the church, the sponsoring church, or the community. Worthwhile community efforts should be supported, and members should not have to make too many difficult choices between competing activities.

The chapel should continue the mission fellowship program. The units should not be discontinued abruptly but should continue as an evangelistic penetration group. Such groups help the congregation to cross more cultural and socioeconomic barriers within the same fellowship. The groups can serve as feeders to the Sunday morning activity and will accelerate growth if conducted carefully.

As the chapel begins, it must seek ways to penetrate its community, providing visible expression of its care and concern for the community. Leaders should remember that one of the foundations of church planting is that love must permeate all that is done. The congregation must provide the salt, light, and leaven for the community in which it has been planted. It must minister Jesus' love in Jesus' name through community ministries and mission action.

Cultivative activities also must remain high on the chapel's priority list. Cultivation follows through on ministry projects and also provides the chapel with active prospects for salvation or membership.

As ministries and cultivation continue, the chapel must be involved in an aggressive visitation program. A good visitation program has two basic elements: people to be visited and people to do the visiting. The pastor and other leaders must provide motivation to the members to visit the lost, the unchurched, the indifferent, and those in need. Motivation is a never-ending process in most mission congregations. However, there is an excitement present in many mission situations which helps to create an atmosphere of evangelistic outreach.

The mission leadership also must maintain an adequate, updated, and well-prepared prospect file. Nothing is more frustrating than for persons to come to church visitation and find they have no one to visit. Likely, they will spurn any future efforts to motivate them to visit.

Research on many slow-growing mission congregations reveals that they invariably have no prospect file. The mission chapel needs to maintain a current church census of its community as the basic source of prospects. To this basic document are added names which have been discovered through cultivative activity, personal contacts, and visitors.

Research of slow-growing mission congregations also has uncovered the basic fact that many of them simply do not visit. An aggressive visitation program includes literally hundreds of calls per month. The pastor must be the point man, doing extensive visitation of prospects on his own and then leading the congregation to share their faith in Jesus Christ.

Good visitation programs normally have at least three basic times for visiting:

• In most churches, visitation night is Thursday night, offering people a stated time for making calls and then for sharing the results and praying for results.

• Daytime visitation, generally in the mornings and usually aimed at housewives;

• Visitation by assignment. Assignments can be given on Sunday, with visitors making calls at their own convenience and returning the cards the following Sunday with the report.

The mission congregation, in its program of church development, must have a leadership training program. New congregations need a definite plan for training leaders. The stability and future growth of the chapel will depend on the leadership that is won, developed, and trained from the new converts who are reached in the new community.

Some Danger Signs

There are some red-warning flags which should be recognized as a new mission chapel is started. The caution signs relate both to the sponsoring church and to the mission congregation.

In the relationship of the sponsoring church to the mission, there is much similarity to that between parent and child. There is absolute necessity to immerse the whole relationship in unselfish love. The Christian hallmark of agape love of seeking the best should permeate the whole relationship. With that as a preface, research indicates several tendencies often arise to threaten that relationship.

First, many times the sponsoring church wants to force the issues for the mission, making decisions and demanding action before the mission is ready. Rather than force these issues, the sponsor should provide opportunities for the new chapel to develop the issues on its own. This, however, takes time, effort, and patience. Again, like the parent and child, the sponsor should allow the "child" to express its feelings and then deal realistically and honestly with them rather than squelching creativity and maturation.

Second, there is a tendency for the mission chapel to want to hang on too long. It seems to want to put off the inevitable. Frightened by its new wings, it hangs on to the security of the nest. The new chapel must come to the point of doing its own thing. That is a point of natural maturation.

Both of these are natural tendencies, and leaders of the sponsor and the chapel should be aware of problems they face if they go too far in either direction.

10. The Financial Issues (Step Seven)

Riverview mission was the outreach congregation of Antioch Church. It met in a rented school building and was experiencing steady, stable growth.

Riverview really wasn't a planned outreach; it just happened. Wyley Brown started the work in the den of his home after he noticed the subdivision in which he lived was experiencing rapid growth. The area—in fact all of Capitol City—was booming.

Antioch's pastor, Frank Boley, went along with the outreach. But it wasn't a real priority with him. The fellowship was largely an effort by Wyley and several of his friends.

When the fellowship reached thirty members, Brown asked the pastor to allow formation into a chapel. With the assent of the congregation, Riverview was started.

Riverview had an active evangelistic visitation program, mainly because most of the members of the chapel were new converts themselves and were eager to see their friends come to know Jesus Christ as their Savior.

Most of the members of the chapel were young, married couples. Because Brown emphasized giving, the collections taken at the chapel each Sunday were very good. The chapel followed denominational guidelines and sent the funds to the treasurer at Antioch.

Most everyone was pleased with the progress of the chapel; it was growing in members and finances. Or so it seemed until Brown got a call from the man who managed the buildings for the Capitol City Independent School District.

"We are concerned because we haven't received the rent check from you people in three months," he told Brown. "We feel we are lenient, but unless we receive the amount you agreed to pay, we will be forced to ask you to leave."

Brown was flabbergasted. He knew offerings were enough to

cover expenses and rent. He put in a hurried call to Pastor Boley. "What's happening?" he wanted to know after he explained.

Boley didn't know but promised to check with the treasurer. He discovered that a separate account had not been established for the mission, but that funds were united into the general fund at the church.

It had been a long summer and attendance at the mother church had slumped. Giving also was down and the treasurer was using the mission fund to take up the slack in the overextended church. He had been using mission offerings to help make the payment on the educational building and to catch up on other bills.

No specific guidelines had been established for him. Therefore, he said, he felt he had a church mandate to use the funds as he saw best. He was more committed to the mother church than to the mission and had taken care of what he assumed were his first priorities.

The misunderstanding enraged the members of Riverview mission. In the heat of anger they called a special business meeting and voted to constitute as a church, and to free themselves from what they thought was indifference toward them and mismanagement of their affairs by Antioch.

The mission formed into a church, but because they were not strong enough to totally support themselves, they had some tight financial squeezes for a while.

Even now, hard feelings between Antioch and Riverview churches still exist.

Church finances, like family, personal, or business finances, can be a blessing or a curse. Carefully handled, finances are a source of pride and accomplishment to a mission chapel. Badly handled, they become a source of debt, disgrace, and hard feelings.

The premise of this book is that finances are not the first consideration. Anytime the idea of starting a new church is mentioned, the most frequent question is: How can it be financed? That should not be the first question. The first priority is reaching people for Christ.

Many of the initial phases of church planting are not expensive; some may not cost anything. Probing into the community in cultivation activities may not cost money. Gasoline for workers involved is often donated. Survey cards are inexpensive and can be produced on a church mimeograph machine. Volunteers can do much of the work.

The establishment of new fellowships, chapels, and churches does not wait on the availability of funds. Ideally, many of the initial activities should be funded by sponsoring churches, assisting churches, or local associations of churches, but funding should not be the initial consideration. We, as Christians, should never forget that God has a way of providing for his work.

When dealing with financing a new work, leaders also should not become afflicted with the "first-class-itis." Inexpensive songbooks often will suffice, as will donated curriculum materials.

Setting the sights on people rather than finances does not mean, however, that leaders of the sponsoring church or the mission congregation should adopt unrealistic attitudes. Fiscal responsibility, integrity, and solvency all are very important in the life of the church. Christians are expected to act even more responsibly with the church's funds than they would with their own personal finances.

Those responsible for the operation of the mission should carefully plan as they determine the financial needs, study the resources available, and manage the money. This, too, is an area where the guidance of the Holy Spirit must be carefully and continuously sought.

Determine the Financial Needs

When talking about starting a new church, one of the most frequent expressions heard around many churches is, "Let's be sure and start it right." Often, this means the sponsor plans to provide generous financial support to launch a new congregation.

However, documented research can be provided to show that mission congregations can become too dependent, much like children who have been given too much by overly benevolent parents. Such dependency inhibits growth and stable development of the new congregation. A welfare syndrome can develop quicker than can a responsible attitude where finances are concerned.

Chapel needs generally are clustered around four considerations: temporary meeting place, leadership, types of ministries to the community, and a permanent location for the new work.

The temporary meeting place generally is the major item in the budget of a mission congregation. Every effort should be made to keep rent to one third or less of the total obligations. Many possibilities exist for controlling this budget item. A full discussion of facilities follows in chapter 11.

Flexibility is imperative in the matter of a meeting place. Such a temporary "home" probably will be far from ideal. It will probably be hard to keep from complaining about all the things that have to be done weekly to make a borrowed or rented building adequate for church use. Hauling materials back and forth can be a hassle, as is setting up and breaking down the arrangement of chairs, dividers, lecturns, and so forth. However, members must be constantly reminded that most of the best things of life take extra time and that the "temporary home" is just that, temporary.

Pastoral leadership is another controlling factor in the financial needs of the church. In most instances, a new congregation does not need a full-time pastor. Often, in the early stages a mission chapel can be led by a competent lay preacher, with the only financial obligation being to pay for his gasoline. Other possibilities are bi-vocational preachers who earn their living from secular employment. Studies indicate the secularly employed pastor of a small church is about as effective as a full-time minister in a similar size congregation. Still another opportunity is offered by retired pastors or denominational workers. Student preachers also should not be overlooked for leadership and supply.

The type of ministry needed in the community should be considered when planning financial needs. In some areas, the nature of the work may demand a full-time pastor from the start. This will make the initial cost much greater.

Occasionally, the pastor of the sponsoring church can serve both churches in the initial stages. In other instances, an organizing pastor could serve a circuit of congregations in an area where several new churches are needed, but none could survive and minister as separate units. As a "field of churches," they can survive and enjoy a less tense and more meaningful existence.

There are few things that can thwart the development of a new chapel more than inadequate finances. This kind of "guilt" feelings should and can be avoided. However, it will take vision, flexibility, and creativity.

As financial needs are planned, mission congregations should look to the future and work at determining their permanent location. In some cases, this will require quick action as land values escalate and needs are great. However, churches have time, generally, to plan adequately and carefully for the future.

Identify the Available Resources

Sources of funds available to most mission congregations fall into three categories; the mission congregation itself, the sponsoring church, and the denominational organization.

One of the foundation blocks in church planting is that "people are basic in church planting." This means people are both the prime resource and the primary target of the church-planting activity. The new congregation, if it has come through some active mission fellowship groups, is made up of new convents and recharged inactive Christians. These people—the nucleus of the congregation—are the primary source of funds.

From the very beginning, biblical concepts of stewardship should be taught, including tithing and full, Christian living. The full Christian life begins with the tithe and goes beyond. The mission congregation should have a steady diet of stewardship—including study courses, stewardship revivals, stewardship lessons in Sunday School, tithing testimonies, tither's commitment day, and many other items. It also should be a year-round emphasis and not one which takes only one week of the year.

Outside assistance should come at the end of the ability of the people to finance the mission and not at the beginning. It should augment the budget, with the members carrying as much of the financial responsibilities as they can and will. Financial support by its members is one of the best indicators of spiritual health in a mission congregation.

Another source of revenue for the fledgling congregation is the sponsoring church. The aid should meet the need. If the sponsoring church—or group of sponsoring churches—must assist with the rent, literature, and pastor's salary, it should do so. However, such aid should be reviewed annually and be on a clearly understood phaseout program.

A third source of funds is from the denomination. Generally, it comes through the local association of churches, regional missions office, or national church extension organization. This assistance is usually for a limited time and is granted on a phaseout basis. The phaseout is designed to foster healthy growth of the mission congregation and aims at building independence rather than fostering dependence.

Manage the Money

At the outset, an agreement and clear understanding needs to be reached on how the money is to be handled. Clear agreements at the beginning limit surprises and embarrassments later.

If the sponsoring church is to handle the money, the arrangement should be agreed to by the mission. It is normally best for the sponsoring church to handle mission funds until the chapel reaches a certain stage of development. At that time, it is part of the training for full church-hood for the mission funds to be handled by a chapel treasurer elected by the sponsoring church.

The mission money should be handled by preparing a detailed and comprehensive budget. The church missions committee, with mission representation, should draft the budget for the chapel, submitting it to the fledgling congregation for reaction. Approval, however, should be from the sponsoring church. Preparation of a budget is good training for the mission congregation.

Careful management of the mission money is required. Safeguards should be instituted and scrupulously adhered to in all stages of dealing with receipts and expenditures. From the time the money is placed in the offering plate, at least two people should be involved in all procedures. Two persons should count the money and certify the amount prior to deposit. The treasurer's checks should always have two signatures when the time comes for the mission to have its own treasurer.

Careful accounting of receipts and expenditures in keeping with budget authorizations or special actions is essential. The treasurer should provide a monthly report of receipts and expenditures to both the mission congregation and to the sponsoring church.

By using proven management techniques and by instituting safeguards, less problems and misunderstandings are likely to occur.

The new congregation also should be encouraged from the first to participate fully in the missionary and benevolent causes of the association, state, or denominational entity to which they belong. This participation is essential to the missionary education development of the new congregation. The budget should specify that a certain percent of all receipts will be given for these causes.

In addition, the special mission offerings—such as those for foreign, home, and state missions—should receive emphasis in the Sunday School, worship service, and prayer meetings.

If the congregation does not participate in such offerings, it can become ingrown and lack worldwide vision. It is a severe mistake for a congregation to wait until it is full grown and has all of its buildings and furnishings before it participates in such benevolence. Such a congregation is self-centered and likely will live as a parasite on the denomination and community of which it is a part.

As mission congregations are managing their finances, there should be a word of caution about the "Installment Plan Disease." A few dollars here and a few dollars there can mount up to be a huge amount if congregations are not careful. Mission congregations have been known to incur debts with printers, florists, grocers, re-pairmen, appliance dealers, music companies, and church supply houses. Often, these debts can escalate far beyond the congregation's ability to pay. The result is fiscal insolvency and disgraceful debt.

Suffice it to say it is much easier to raise money before a project is begun than it is to do so afterwards.

11. Provide Facilities (Step Eight)

William Brock was bubbling with enthusiasm as he entered Jay Taylor's office. Visions of lovely, huge, white-columned church buildings danced before his eyes.

Brock had come to the headquarters of his denomination to apply for a loan to buy ten acres of property and build a $250,000 building in Apple Valley to house his mission congregation.

Taylor, who was head of the denominations loan program for church sites and buildings, thought wearily, "Oh, no. Not another one."

Taylor patiently began to question the visionary young pastor. "How many people live in Apple Valley?" he queried. "Population of the town is 3,000, but Lincoln County has a population of over 6,000," answered Brock.

"How many people do you plan to be able to seat in your sanctuary?" Taylor questioned.

"We are planning for about 750," Brock replied.

"How many members do you have now?" Taylor asked.

"We are running about sixty in worship service right now," Brock responded.

Taylor, who had been through the entire process before with visionary young pastors, began to try to show Brock that he was overplanning and overestimating the capability of the small mission chapel at Apple Valley.

"Many young pastors vastly overestimate community response to their churches," Taylor began. "Many of them unfortunately don't plan well and saddle chapel congregations with huge debts. . . ."

The encounter droned on and on, with Taylor trying to help Brock understand. Brock, his head crammed full of visions of white columns and huge steeples, didn't understand.

He was vastly disappointed with the recommendation that the church build a small first unit capable of seating 100 people on a smaller site.

"He simply didn't understand the difference between dreams and realities," Taylor said sadly.

The facility is a tool in church planting; it is not an end in itself. That fact must remain in sharp focus as facilities for mission congregations are considered.

Christ established a church that had no property or any permanent meeting place. He dispatched the seventy out two by two on a mission of ministry and witness to people. If he were sending them out today, within a week or two, several of the disciples would show up and say, "Lord, I want to show you a choice piece of property."

Jesus emphasized evangelizing people. He did not promote surveying real estate. The early disciples had temporary facilities in which to meet. They met in homes, synagogues, by the seashore, and in the upper room. The message, not the facility, was the crucial issue to them. Any place was fine, so long as they could tell others about Jesus.

With the growth of Christianity, facilities have become a helpful tool in worship and Christian education. But we must ever be mindful that the facility is an instrument to be used in the propagation of the gospel. The church is not the building; the church is the people of God on mission to the world.

The foundational block of church planting that "people are basic" must always be kept in mind. Facilities are important, but they are to be used as tools and not revered as shrines.

The place of property or facilities in church planting today varies in keeping with the community where the church is going to be planted. In areas of booming growth and rapid expansion, obtaining sites for churches obviously is of high priority. Many denominational organizations have established site funds to provide assistance and/or sites in such rapidly growing areas. In those cases, prices are a main consideration, and sites must be obtained before costs soar too high.

In other areas, however, scarcity of available land and high prices is not the key concern. The ideal process is for the mission chapel to start services in a temporary facility and remain there until sufficient stability and strength has been established. Mission congregations should have a minimum of a dozen families who are permanent residents and fully committed to the chapel before embarking on serious consideration of obtaining permanent facilities.

Temporary Facilities

Two-car garages, basements, dens, recreation rooms, and even patios and lawns have provided a site for new chapels.

An Example: Oakridge chapel began in the living room of Wayne and Loretta Cousins in Sandy Beach. It started with only six people, but within two months it had outgrown the living room and moved into the garage. In six months, the chapel was moved to a double-wide mobile home and the congregation began looking for property. Within two years, the growing chapel purchased a two-acre site and built a simple first-unit building.

Almost any facility can be used to house an embryo congregation. Storefronts are used but often are criticized by persons who have little or no experience in church planting. Several hundred new churches are planted each year in America in store buildings. Many grow into strong, effective churches. When available, storefronts make effective and useful sites to temporarily house mission congregations.

Some school districts make their buildings available. Hundreds of missions use auditoriums, which are vacant on Sunday, as sites for their worship services. In some areas, declining elementary enrollments have forced school consolidation, and vacant buildings are available for church use. Charges often are nominal.

Church buildings also are available, and rental normally is scarcely more than utilities would be. Seventh-Day Adventist churches frequently are obtainable, and many mainline denominations offer their buildings at alternate hours. Rising costs of heat and utilities make many churches open to assistance on the costs of fuel and electricity.

An Example: Copper Valley chapel was started in a prayer group in the Lincoln Hotel by two men. Soon, they were reaching out into the community of 19,000 and were averaging three couples—eleven people—and six college students. There was no other church of their denomination within a 100-mile radius, and the small group decided to begin Sunday services. They rented a Seventh-Day Adventist church building in the community, for which they pay $25 per Sunday. The small congregation now is looking for a full-time pastor to help build the church and its ministry throughout Copper Valley and Copper County. They are satisfied with their arrangement and have negotiated with the Seventh-Day Adventist congregation to remain in the building until growth surpasses the facilities.

Many other facilities are available to mission congregations as temporary sanctuary. Motel conference rooms, hotel parlors, community buildings, lodges, club rooms, and others are good places to meet. The cost is low, and the facilities generally acceptable.

Mission congregations and members of the sponsoring church should carefully avoid rushing into locating permanent facilities for the outreach group. Cramped facilities often are preferable to the agony of heavy indebtedness and financial strain.

Site Purchase

Church-planting workers should concentrate their activities on reaching people, but while they are people searching, they also can be alert to good site possibilities. During the fellowship and chapel stages, the members can be the eyes and ears for good site possibilities.

When seeking sites, several items should be kept in mind.

1. *Topography.*—The land ought to have good drainage and be mostly level. It should contain a large enough level area for parking and the site should be compatible with the type of building which the congregation can afford.

2. *Zoning.*—The zoning ordinances must be checked to find out local requirements. Persons responsible for seeking the site should be familiar with the city zoning ordinance and its provisions as they relate to churches. Churches can be stymied by parking requirements which require a certain number of spaces in ratio to attendance. Unfamiliarity with zoning ordinances can cause difficulties for the unaware congregation.

The zoning law usually requires specified set backs from the property line, and landscaping sometimes is specified. Codes often govern building height, and these structure requirements can make chapel construction prohibitive in certain areas.

3. *The future.*—A check with city or county planning commission workers is advised. The planners may know of some proposed construction project in the area which may make a potential site undesirable. They may know of plans which would enhance the likelihood of church growth in a different sector.

92 PLANTING NEW CHURCHES

4. *Government.*—Paving assessments, curbing, water, or sewer lines, basements, and the like can cause grief to the unwary. One struggling mission chapel was staggered when the community hit them with a huge assessment for paving streets on three sides and installing water and sewer lines.

5. *Other churches.*—The proximity of sister churches should be considered when selecting a site. Normally, geographic dispersion is desirable, although nearby churches can minister to separate socioeconomic or cultural strata. Other churches of very similar denominations with similar worship styles or programs should be considered when locating church sites. If a new church can have its own community to serve with its own particular persuasion and worship style, it generally will grow faster and have a more effective witness and ministry.

6. *Site fund.*—Mission congregations would do well to establish a site fund and earmark a portion of their income for that purpose. Such a portion should be included in the budget of the congregation, and planning for the future should be a regular part of any fiscal policy of the congregation. To promote the site fund, special envelopes should be designed and made available in the pews and offering plates. Special mention should be made of the opportunity for over-and-above gifts to the site fund. Many mission congregations have established that the fifth Sunday offerings will be used primarily for the site fund.

Mission congregations which have established such a site fund often find it advisable to invest the funds in savings certificates with banks or savings institutions, thus allowing their money to earn money while they prepare for their permanent location.

Many denominations have site-loan funds available to mission congregations. Often, these funds are interest free for a period of two or three years. If these funds can be obtained and used to purchase sites, the congregation may wish to hold the land and pay off the fund before beginning any building program. Thus, the burden of debt may be much less if the congregation undertakes the project in segments.

The Church Building

The ego needs and impractical dreams of many organizing pastors have caused many new congregations to overbuild their first unit building. Often it looks like a warehouse at the rear of the church site.

An Example: Hillcrest Mission purchased a lovely site on the outskirts of Bayou City. The building committee decided a two-story, rectangular building should be the first unit.

"We could use it as sanctuary and Sunday School space and it would remodel easily into a first-rate educational building when we get ready to build the sanctuary," they told the church.

The funds were borrowed and the church accepted a large debt. But the church did not grow as rapidly as planners thought, and twenty years later, the many church members refer to the old barracks-looking building as a "monstrosity."

Mission congregations are urged to make their first units attractive, while building in features which will make expansion possible. The first unit buildings should be completed with no unfinished aspects.

Jesus told a parable about counting the cost before beginning a building. Many churches have forgotten Christ's advice and have become a laughingstock in their community because of uncompleted buildings.

As they plan for first units churches should be constantly aware of the possibility of multiple worship services and multiple Sunday School classes. If such possibility isn't part of the initial plan, it is doubtful it will ever be accepted as part of any plan.

A lovely and well-appointed church building will help develop and maintain a good church program of community ministry, but the building will not initiate the program. The building will be helpful in attracting people, but scores of people won't break down the doors just because the church has a nice, attractive building. The building is only a tool, and the workers must be committed to use it as such.

For many denominational agencies, reaching the lost is the key consideration in determining loans to churches. Robert H. Kilgore, director of the Division of Church Loans for the Southern Baptist Home Mission Board, has said that collateral for a church loan is the church's program and that program's capacity to reach and develop people for Christ. Real estate values, he says, are of secondary concern.

A church's programs are but a reflection of a church's understanding of its mission. As long as the church is more concerned about people and their needs than about structure and its visibility, then the structures will be a means to an end and not the end. Such an understanding is imperative if the church is to be what God intends it to be.

When a church is planning a building program, it should seek to determine its future maximum size and plan accordingly. Kilgore, whose division deals with more than 2,000 congregations annually, thinks it is possible to predict accurately community response to a church.

Community response to church programs are based on a grouping of six factors, Kilgore believes. The issue has been proven in a number of surveys and intensive studies made of churches and church fields. The prediction is based primarily on the community in which the church is located as well as the type of ministry and program reflected by the church.

"There is no such thing as a church with unlimited growth," Kilgore says. "All have limiting factors and a church should find these limiting factors and plan its opportunities within the framework of its limitations."

Factors which limit growth are geographical, cultural, racial, leadership (lay and pastoral), theological, and economic.

As an instance, church growth frequently is limited by such geographical boundaries as rivers, limited access superhighways, railroads, and industrial districts. When a new highway is constructed through a community, it divides the area, and people who live on one side generally will not attend church on the other.

Communities also reflect growth cycles, and churches which ignore such factors do so at their own peril. The American Society of Real Estate Appraisers reports that every community undergoes four stages: growth, stabilization, transition, and renewal. Normally, it takes fifty years for a community to go through this cycle, but in today's world, some communities have undergone the entire cycle in ten years.

Churches generally reach a cultural community within geographical boundaries and attendance cycles follow closely the community population cycle. In other words, the church reflects its community.

For instance, shopping center developers indicate the average age of the average shopping center in the nation is fifteen years. After that initial period, the name stores move out and secondary stores move in. As time passes, the once magnificent shopping center becomes nondescript and has many vacant shops. As the shopping center has evolved, the community around it also has undergone transition, moving from higher to lower socioeconomic strata.

Churches, however, do not heed the advice of commercial builders. Studies have indicated that churches started in the same communities with the shopping malls usually build magnificent sanctuaries and seemingly expect to go on forever. When transition occurs, however, many churches are left with huge debts which their current constituents can't handle.

Churches should plan their building by small units, with provision for expansion as the need arises. Each unit should have the appearance of a completed project. Churches should keep debt payment small enough so that a program of ministry can be provided. The building should not absorb all of the time, energies, and finances of the members. The church is there to serve its members; not vice versa. If suitable programs cannot be provided, the church is not needed anyway.

It is strongly urged that no more than one third of anticipated income be committed to debt retirement. If the proportion is larger than one third to two thirds, the program is out of balance.

Many denominations offer consultants for church building. Many offer plans and expertise in planning and constructing the building. (For a sample of several building plans, see Appendices F, G, and H.) Many costly mistakes can be averted by using the available counsel of such consultants.

The purchase of a church site and construction of a first-unit building can either kill or cure the new congregation. If the debt is prohibitive and suffocating, it will depress the spirit of the church and eliminate all joy and praise in worship. The atmosphere of strain also will prohibit new people from joining the new congregation. Also, overbuilding causes the people to sit forlornly in the massive sanctuary "rattling around like a pea in a boxcar." The unfilled seats depress pastor and people and inhibit growth. A well-filled small church is far better, psychologically, than is a desolate and empty large building.

Mission congregations considering building new facilities should seek every shred of counsel and expertise on the matter. An old sermon on church buildings was called "The Building Sets the Pattern." It certainly does—to growth and vitality or to gloom and depression.

12. Constitute the Church (Step Nine)

It was a big day for Springdale Mission. On this day they were to become Springdale Church.

There hadn't been much time to plan, it had all happened very quickly. Only two weeks before lay pastor Philip Baldwin announced, "Let's constitute into a church."

The idea was met with immediate favor and the members wanted to do it soon. They knew it should be a big day, and they decided on a date. They had a lot of trouble finding a speaker. The state executive for their denomination was going to be out of the state on that Sunday. His assistant couldn't come; he already had agreed to preach a revival downstate. The missions director likewise was committed.

They tried to get the state newspaper editor to appear, but he couldn't come. When they got down to their regional office, they found the director of missions and all of the staff members were tied up that Sunday.

They finally found a speaker, but no one was really satisfied. They wanted the day they formed into a church to be a BIG day.

When the day came, it was as big a fiasco as had been their hurried attempts to find a speaker. Nobody remembered to call the newspaper and the preacher forgot about calling the florist until Saturday afternoon. No press coverage; no flowers.

There was no program for their big day; it really turned out to be a flop.

Instead of looking back on the day as a milestone in the life of the congregation, everybody remembered the depressing Sunday that was supposed to be a BIG day in the life of Springdale Church.

The day a mission becomes a church should be a high, holy, and spiritual event in the life of the mission and of its sponsor. It should come in the fullness of time—when the church and the mission feel it is ready—and it should be an event to remember.

Formal constitution of a mission congregation into a self-governing church should be deferred until everyone concerned is convinced the group is spiritually mature and sufficiently stable to govern themselves. Countless instances can be cited of mission churches which died because they were constituted prematurely.

Two specific instances come to mind: One church had seventy-three charter members when it was constituted, yet it died within three months because of the instability of the leadership. Another was formed into a self-governing organization with eighty charter members; it was dead within a year. It could not survive without the mature counsel and leadership of the church missions committee of the sponsoring church.

There seems to be a definite relationship between the manner of starting a new church and the readiness with which it congeals into a good, vigorous congregation that is able to fulfill its mission to the world.

What Constituting a Church Means

Constituting a chapel into a church brings into being a new legal and spiritual identity. With constituting, a mission becomes a separate, spiritual unit, creating and generating spiritual resources and ministries.

Constituting signifies that the chapel has grown into a stable church.

Constituting into a church makes the mission congregation more self-determining. It is forced to assume responsibility for its own obligations and to make its own decisions.

Constituting into a church helps the new congregation make giant steps toward maturity. As long as some other church has ultimate responsibility, the mission has less maturity. When responsiblity is assumed by the local group, a greater degree of maturity is required.

Constituting a mission chapel into a church is an important step, signifying the congregation has come of age and is ready to assume its role as minister and witness to the unchurched and inactive people who live in it's field.

When Do We Constitute?

It is impossible to set a definite timetable on when a chapel will be ready to become a church, but several guidelines should be considered.

First, it is time to constitute when the mission congregation has come into a sense of fellowship with Jesus Christ and each other. There is real spiritual unity and love. The group feels they are truly the family of God. If there are serious problems which could mar this fellowship and indicate disruption within the body, constitution should be deferred. It is only after a church has jelled into a unit that constitution should be considered.

Second, it is time to constitute the mission into a new church when the people have come to perceive the biblical basis for why they have come together. Constitution should come only after the church has developed a true sense of identity and of mission. They know why the mission was started and are willing to shoulder that responsibility. They have developed a "mission design" by which they propose to achieve the purpose of God for the new church. It is only after a chapel has come to know and to feel deeply that they are God's people at work in the world that they should form a new church.

Third, it is time to constitute the mission into a new church when the people have become aware of community needs, of the challenge in their field, and they have a vision of the potential of the field in which their church has been planted. When they can see the need, when they know that under God's leadership something can be done to meet that need, and when they know deep in their hearts that God has commissioned them to work toward meeting that need they should constitute into a new church.

Fourth, it is time to constitute a new church when the membership of the chapel has become numerically and financially adequate to perform the ministry needed in the community. Some experts feel 100 members is the minimum number for initial membership, but the exact number may vary in keeping with the abilities and resources of the congregation. Nevertheless, many mission congregations constitute with too few members to be effective in reaching and witnessing to their field.

Fifth, it is time to constitute if the mission congregation has had adequate training in church polity, Christian doctrine, stewardship, and in the various methods needed by various offices to perform their tasks.

A deliberate and consciously prepared training program to achieve these goals should be planned and executed before constitution occurs. This is preventive maintenance, which is always more effective and less expensive than crisis management.

Sixth, it is time to constitute if the mission congregation has become self-supporting and is able to phase out all outside help. It is not good stewardship to continue giving denominational assistance to a weak church when it could be channeled through a strong sponsoring church with a functioning church missions committee.

Preparing to Constitute

Constitution of a church is an event which should be as carefully planned and prepared as a president's inauguration. It is an important event in the life of the church and should be prayerfully and carefully developed.

First, the mission should formally request permission to constitute from the sponsoring church. The application, as well as all ensuing activities, should be done with consultation and counsel of the church missions committee of the sponsor. If the application is approved, preparation can continue.

The date should be carefully chosen. It should be set far enough in advance so that key denominational officials and press representatives may be present. Information should be provided to the news media far enough in advance to provide good news coverage of the event. The church also may wish to retain a photographer to make pictures of the historic event for their own records.

A constitution committee should be appointed to write a church constitution and bylaws. This should be planned several months in advance in order to give the church an opportunity to participate in the creation of the document under which it will govern itself.

The committee should research the matter of constitutions, contacting regional or national church administration offices. Constitutions of sister churches also should be studied.

The constitution, when written, should include these items:
- A preamble setting forth the purpose of the constitution.
- The name of the church. This becomes the official, legal title. If the church is incorporated under this name, no other church can legally use that name in the state.
- The purposes of the church
- A church doctrinal statement (The Articles of Faith)
- The church covenant

- The government and polity of the church
- Its denominational affiliation, local, state, regional, national
- The procedure by which it can be amended

The bylaws should include material relating to membership, officers, committees, organizations, ordinances, meetings, and other general procedural matters.

The new church should plan to incorporate so it can become a legal entity, protecting individual members or officers from personal liability for accidents and debts. Incorporation provides many advantages and is relatively simple to accomplish.

After the date has been set and the constitution committee has done its work, the church missions committee and the chapel steering committee should invite neighboring churches, denominational, and civic leaders to attend the constituting service.

The service, like the many steps along the way, should be planned under the leadership and direction of the Holy Spirit. It should not be slammed together at the last minute but should be lovingly prepared as a great event. There are many options, but a sample constituting service may include:

Hymn: "The Church's One Foundation"
Scripture: Matt. 16:18–19; Acts 2:41–42; 1 Cor. 12:27; Eph. 4:11–13; Col. 1:18
Recommendations from the sponsoring church *
Motion to formally constitute the church *
Election of officers and committees *

Presentation of the title to the property *
Motion to incorporate *
Adoption of constitution and bylaws *
Hymn: "To God Be the Glory"
Offering for missions
Sermon: "The Mission of the Church"
Invitation for new members
Reception of new members
Benediction

* These items should have been thoroughly worked through by the mission congregation so that actual adoption is perfunctory and all discussion was done prior to the formal service.

If carefully prepared and carried out, the constitution service will have intense meaning. And churches, like all God's children, need milestones along the way for guidance and encouragement.

13. The Nine Steps and Denominational Concerns

Nathan Dudley was area director of missions in the Yardley-Wellington association of churches, composed of thirty-seven churches in a two-county area. Dudley knew there were many needs in this area, including the need to plant new churches in rapidly growing areas.

One of the best ways to meet those needs, he felt, was the encourage the members of the association to elect church missions committees. Dudley devised a promotional plan to encourage response. He mailed out information, inserted blurbs in the monthly bulletin, had special recognition of churches with church missions committees, and did many other things to help churches see the need.

After several months, fifteen of the churches had elected church missions committees. Dudley compiled a mailing list of the chairmen of these committees and began a program of mailing helpful information, manuals, booklets, leaflets, and studies. He scheduled a banquet for the members of the fifteen committees, along with their pastors. During the fete, he showed the movie Planned Parenthood for Churches and had the chairmen of the most effective committees tell how their committee functioned.

Later, Dudley scheduled a retreat for the committees, giving intensive training by using visuals, lectures, study groups, and discussions. He invited the churches which had not elected committees to send a "good, mission-minded person" to the retreat.

The promotional-informational plan was not a short-term thing; Dudley planned that the emphasis on the church missions committee would continue.

Finally, his work paid off. Statistics indicated that many of the churches had established new work.

After four years of effort, there was a 20 percent increase in the number of churches in the association. By using the church

*missions committee as a base, motivator, research group, and
guide, the thirty-seven churches in the association had planted
seven new churches reaching many people in the growing areas
of the two-county sector.*

The preceding nine chapters have discussed the nine steps of
church planting in detail. However, much of the thrust was aimed
at the local church or the local pastor. In each of the steps, there
are concerns and responsibilities which relate to denominational
leaders, whether associational, district, regional, state, or national.

The Church Missions Committee (Step One)

Denominational leaders who desire to efficiently accelerate new
church development in their area of responsibility need to encourage churches to elect church missions committees. To do this, they
need to devise a promotional plan to help churches see the need
and to understand a method by which the need can be met.

The denominational workers should encourage formation of such
committees and then develop mailing lists to be used regularly as
a method of prodding the committee to function. Training events—
such as banquets, retreats, study courses, and so forth—need to be
included in the denominational calendar.

Good training material should be identified and secured. There
are a number of motion-picture films, filmstrips, manuals, study
course books, and planned presentations which can be obtained
for use in such training.

Rather than being only trainers, the denominational leaders also
should avail themselves of all training opportunities, seeking to be
as well prepared as possible for their work. If the denominational
worker is prepared, he can serve as a resource person for the local
committees.

Select Areas for New Work (Step Two)

Much of the discussion in chapter 5 is relevant for denominational
leaders, and they are encouraged to study it carefully. In addition,
denominational leaders should be a guide to the larger fellowship
of churches to cooperate in a region-wide survey of new work needs,
gathering data, preparing maps, taking surveys, studying the overall
picture, and setting priorities related to the needs.

John H. Allen, in the *Church Extension Planbook* has devised a series of thirteen questions by which a regional missions committee can rate new work needs and arrive at a rather "scientific" setting of priorities on a numerical basis. (See Appendix C for the score sheet and instructions on scoring priorities.)

Allen's questions:

1. What is the population of the community?

2. What is the ratio of unchurched and/or unevangelized in the community?

3. What was the response to previous attempts to evangelize the community? High? Low?

4. What is the potential influence of the community for Christ and his kingdom, such as capital city, county seat, university, resort area.

5. Is it strategic to denominational growth in future outreach as a base or outpost?

6. Consider its world mission or evangelism influence. It may be that because of a military base, diplomatic station, university, etc., the people will scatter from this point to the far regions of the world.

7. What is the availability of the community to be self-supporting in the least possible time?

8. Analyze the missions resource necessary to establish the work and give priority to those requiring the least resources with the greatest potential.

9. What communities are within the reach and availability of the local established churches for their sponsorship? Rate the degree of involvement.

10. What communities can be "paired in a church field" with other churches or new church field opportunities?

11. Is there, at present, a mission nucleus active in the community that has gathered some disciples together? If so, are they seeking to develop the fellowship into a church?

12. Are personnel available to go to these areas; do they feel God is leading them to a particular place?

13. Does the community have other acceptable alternatives for evangelization other than establishing a new church?

A very real part of intelligent selection of areas for new work involves a community survey to ascertain specific religious data:

the number of unchurched, religious preferences, inactive persons of various denominations.

The associational or regional director of missions, working with his missions committee, can set dates for volunteer survey workers from all of the churches to survey a particular community.

An Example: When I was an associational director of missions, we decided to survey a community of 15,000. We set the date for Saturday, and thirty volunteers came from nine churches and missions. We met at the city park, under the tabernacle. There, we made assignments, which were drawn in detail on the 5" by 7" envelopes. We also instructed the survey workers in how to complete the cards, suggested methods of approach, cautioned them to avoid religious discussions, and encouraged them to make good impressions.

From 10:00 A.M. to 4:00 P.M. we surveyed the entire eastern half of the city. We discovered the names, addresses, ages, telephone numbers, and other vital information on 1,800 prospects.

A month later, we started a new congregation. From the survey we discovered that the Eastern section of the city was the proper place for a new mission. Subsequent growth of the mission demonstrated the validity of the selection. Within a year the church was self-supporting.

When surveying the communities, denominational leaders are urged to use a family survey card. (See Appendix D.)

The survey also can be taken by telephone, using the same card. People with good telephone voices are most desirable. (For instructions for telephone canvassers, see Appendix E.)

After working through the questions listed in chapter 5, establishing a list of places exposed through the thirteen priority-setting questions, and setting the priority list, the denominational leader and his missions committee should bring the recommendations through the process of approval by executive boards of the association, district, region, or state for their concurrence. This brings into play one of the foundation blocks of church planting: "Participation planning is essential to effective church planting."

Preparing the Sponsoring Church (Step Three)

Before a pastor of lay leadership will lead their church in preparing to sponsor new work, they must also be motivated and interested.

"Not one of my pastors is interested in starting a new church," said Duane Norman, associational director of missions for the Northway association. "I can't even get them to talk about new work. They feel they have all they can do in just growing their own churches."

Norman then made the plea: "What can I do?"

I had been asked to visit Duane, look at his field, and make some suggestions. We traveled around the associational area for three days. It was obvious to me: He had a glaring need for new churches.

Finally, at noon on the third day, I asked to see his associational calendar. It was, as always, jam-packed with too many meetings.

Looking closely, I saw the weekly pastor's conference. I asked Norman what sort of program he scheduled, and he replied: "Not much of anything. Just coffee, statistical reports, and the like. Sometimes we have a guest speaker."

I suggested he arrange for some guest speakers to bring motivational messages on missions. I also advised him to prepare a visual presentation on new work needs to share with the pastors.

We looked at other meetings, and saw there were many programs where messages, filmstrips, movies, and testimonies about church planting could be inserted into the existing agenda.

Together, we readied a year of preparation for the pastors and lay leaders of the Northway association.

In many cases, the denominational leader is a key factor in one of the foundations of church planting: "Creating a suitable climate is essential to effective church planting." The leader can give intensive attention to devising a plan to create such a climate of awareness that the local church leadership will be motivated to begin new work.

One of the ways the associational or regional director can create this awareness is through assembling intelligent research data which presents the need. He also can appeal to the hearts of those with whom he works, detailing how they can be more effective in reaching people for Jesus Christ.

Cultivating the Mission Field (Step Four)

Each summer across America, hundreds of youth choirs and youth mission teams seek places to serve. According to Southern Baptist Home Mission Board figures, more than 15,000 young people of this one denomination seek mission opportunities each summer.

Most of these teams could be used in cultivating new work areas with choir concerts, dramas, puppet shows, Backyard Bible Clubs, Vacation Bible Schools, recreation programs, and many other things.

An Example: Dialing his telephone, Joe Moore inquired: "Say, Al, could you use a youth puppet team for your missions project sometime in the next few weeks? I just talked to Marvin Haynes in the Northern part of the state, and he told me his youth puppet group wants to make a short trip and be involved in some mission project."

Moore was talking with Al Dodge, director of missions of the Twin Forks association, who was seeking to cultivate a new work area in Smithfield. Such a puppet team was just what he needed to help conduct Backyard Bible Clubs in the El Camino subdivision.

Moore and Dodge worked out the details. In three weeks, Haynes and the young people from First Church arrived. They had a place to stay, an area to cultivate, and some recreational activities. It was a good experience for the youth, their sponsors, and for the director of missions who needed help in cultivating the area.

Alert directors of missions will find hundreds of opportunities to use youth groups in community cultivation. The denominational leader can be the funnel through which volunteers come to new work areas. He also can guide and assist churches who are interested in receiving the volunteer help.

However, the denominational leader must be prepared to work hard to make necessary arrangements and to be the facilitator and implementor of such activities.

Some denominational offices provide bookmobiles on a periodic basis, assisting in the cultivation of new areas with the roving, lending library. Other mobile recreation units—Fun Wagons—also are being used to attract children and young people. Often such recreation vehicles are built and equipped in more established areas and provided free of charge—some even with personnel to staff them during summer months—to new work areas.

Such items as youth groups, bookmobiles, and Fun Wagons are useful in doing community cultivation and in building bridges to people. Populous areas with many potential new-work areas might do well to secure these kinds of resources to provide to their churches on a periodic basis.

The Mission Fellowship (Step Five)

Denominational leaders in an association or region can provide workshops to train lay leaders to lead the mission fellowships.

An Example: Harry Carter of the Jefferson County association of churches scheduled a "Mission Fellowship Institute" for the forty-three churches in the area. He discovered that many of the churches interested in starting new work through a mission fellowship only had two or three people to train and did not feel it was necessary to have a workshop to train such a small number of people.

Carter laid his plans for the workshop institute well in advance, scheduling church extension, Sunday School, and church training workers from the state office as speakers. He prepared a detailed notebook for each of the participants, including resource materials, suggested helps, and a recommended reading list.

He enlisted the pastors of the association, who recruited their interested workers.

Carter even offered box lunches of fried chicken for the participants and set the agenda so there would be ample time for feedback and personal conferences.

Because of his preparation, fifty workers in the Jefferson County association received the best information, resources, and training possible.

Leaders of associational or regional denominational offices can be resource persons to train and lead the work in establishing mission fellowships. They can add impetus to the movement toward launching new work.

The Emerging Congregation (Steps Six through Nine)

The denominational leader closest to the local church could be a tremendous resource person to help the local church as it launches the mission chapel. He could have material and information readily at hand to facilitate many aspects of starting the mission congregations.

He could provide, for example:

• Sample bylaws for the mission chapel which outline the relationship between the fledgling congregation and the sponsoring church.

• Information sheets on handling finances.

- Sample floor plans of first unit buildings, and the proper contacts for good building counsel.
- Data on funds available for building and/or site purchase, including sources of counsel on church debt.
- Specific information for legal incorporation of the new congregation into a nonprofit corporation. In many states, a simple form from the state secretary of state, along with a fee, is all that is required for incorporation. Such information could save the churches hundreds of dollars in legal fees.
- Sample constitutions.
- Suggestions for constituting services.

Hopefully, denominational offices will see themselves as key factors in new work. The leaders of the associational or regional office can be facilitators and implementors, easing the way and helping to remove roadblocks.

The leaders should study the nine steps and provide files for each of them, accumulating pertinent information as a ready resource to the churches as needed.

There are many ways in which denominational leaders can be involved in planting new churches. But they must be alert to the possibilities, ready to give such efforts a high priority, prepared to work hard, and predisposed to seek the leadership and guidance of the Holy Spirit.

SECTION III

The Mission Pastor

14. Important Perspectives for Mission Pastors

David Lewis was very unhappy; what's more, he was very frustrated. He had been pastor of Newtown Church for three years. In fact, he was the only pastor the small, struggling Northern church had ever had. He had worked to cultivate the community and to plant the church. After three years, there were sixty members in the church, and the congregation had a small building on the main street of the 10,000 population town.

But Lewis was frustrated. "Things are just puttering along," he told his wife, Anne. "We're pouring our life into this church and who cares? We've worked and worked and worked, and it just seems like a dead end."

What David didn't tell Anne was that he had been thinking about his friends from college and seminary days—friends who were pastoring successful churches in the South. "They're doing good," he told himself. "We went to the same schools, learned the same things, and studied from the same books. They're doing good; what's wrong with me?"

Lewis had a classic case of the blues. He felt sorry for himself, and thought he was a failure.

But David began to pray. He set aside an hour each morning to seek God and find some answer for his struggle. As he prayed, a growing sense of newness surrounded him. He had doubted whether God had really sent him to Newtown to start the new mission.

But as he prayed, David's sense of call began to grow. He knew he was God's man, called to preach and to teach and to win people to Jesus. What's more, he had regained his sense that not only was he God's man, but that he was God's man in Newtown.

And, as he prayed, his sense of calling grew. Simultaneously, his unhappiness and frustration disappeared as he sought to do God's work where he was.

To be effective—and happy—a mission pastor must have a sense of his calling; he must be possessed by it and constantly aware that he is God's man. The mission pastor must be compelled, impelled, and driven to his task. He must know in his heart that he cannot be anything but a preacher.

As the mission pastor embarks on a difficult and sometimes painful life, he must keep a tight grip on who he is, and to whom he is related. He must know beyond a shadow of a doubt that God has called him.

The mission pastor must be able to think back to that time when he became convinced, beyond questioning, that God was calling him into the preaching ministry, the pastoral ministry.

We all need milestones in our Christian life, a specific time and event to recall, to remember, to think on. Those milestones can be to our lives like transformers are to electrical lines, placed at regular intervals to give a new surge of energy and power, pushing the electricity down the wire.

So it is with the mission pastor. That remembrance of his calling must be a milestone—a transformer—in his life, giving a needed surge of energy. When we are certain who we are, certain that God has called us into his service, we can face frustrations and challenges with additional strength.

The mission pastor must be able to look back on his call and remember when the Holy Spirit so possessed his mind and heart and being, telling him in every fiber of his body that God wanted him to preach the gospel.

This fundamental, basic sense of calling is essential to the life of the mission pastor as he considers who he is and what he is doing.

Not only must the mission pastor be aware of his calling, he also must be aware of his calling to new church development. There is a great difference between being pastor of an established church which has been in operation for generations, with established leadership, resources, and facilities, and accepting the leadership of a new mission congregation which is still seeking able leadership, resources, and facilities. The first church is entrenched and well-founded; the other is struggling to establish its very existence.

The mission pastor, to be effective, must be sure that God has called him to the work of new church development. He cannot serve effectively if he is unsure of his divine call to such work.

Once the mission pastor has become aware of his call to the ministry and of his call to new work, he must seek God's will about the specific place of service. The mission pastor should serve where he feels God has placed him.

Serving a new church is somewhat like starting a marriage. In the marriage there must be a commitment and a dedication to the partner. There must be a determination to stick it out through thick and thin. One of the reasons many marriages fail is because there is no sense of commitment to the partner. One of the reasons many mission pastors fail is because they have no sense of calling and commitment to the specific place of service.

The mission pastor must be fully aware that God has called him to *THAT* place, to *THAT* church, to *THAT* congregation, and that it is God's will that he serve there. If the pastor isn't fully aware of the specific call of God, he cannot serve effectively. He will have a limited, ineffective ministry.

To be effective, the mission pastor must be aware of who he is— that he is God's man, called of the Lord to be a minister and a pastor. He must know God has called him into a special sort of ministry—new church development. And, he must know that God has called him specifically to a certain place to do pioneer missions work.

The mission pastor must also sense the needs of the community; he must be aware of the unchurched, the lost. The mission pastor must know that people who do not have Jesus Christ as their personal Savior are lost, apart from God, aliens. This knowledge of how awful lostness is must pull on his heart; he must ache for the lost.

He also must know that he, as God's man, has been sent to that community to be a minister of reconciliation, to help them accept the reconciliation that God has provided through Christ.

He must take a close look at his field. He should be aware of the unchurched. He also must know of the unenlisted people who formerly were active in some Christian church but who have dropped out along the way. Unenlisted Christians cover the nation by multitudes. Such people are prospects for any church who can rekindle their sleeping faith and enlist them back into Christian service.

As the mission pastor takes a close look at his community, he should see the total human needs of people. He must see the hurt, and how he can help, see loneliness and how he can be a friend, see need and how he can be a blessing.

To be effective, the mission pastor must know and love his field. He must be aware of the great human need which exists there: unchurched, unenlisted people who need ministry which he, as God's man, can provide.

The mission pastor, to be effective, must know the work of the minister. A study of the minister and his work in the Scriptures should kindle a fire of mission in his heart, because, first of all, the work of the ministry is the work of Christ.

Christ, himself, told the disciples, "As my Father hath sent me, even so send I you" (John 20:21). Christ came on a mission of redemption, which he completed in his death on Calvary, redeeming that which was lost and apart from God. He came on a mission of revelation, to show the world that God is kind, loving, and compassionate; that he is concerned about his creation. Christ came on a mission of reconciliation, to bring man to God. This work of reconciliation has been entrusted to us, God's people. Reconciliation already has been completed. Jesus reconciled man and God; it is the church's task in the world today to minister that reconciliation to all peoples.

Christ also came to bind up the brokenhearted and to set the captives free. And, in this mission also, he leaves to the church the work of being the messenger of comfort, of hope, of encouragement. God's people must seek out workers to proclaim: "Ye shall know the truth, and the truth shall make you free." He sends out his ministers to shout from the housetops: "If the Son therefore shall make you free, ye shall be free indeed." He has sent his church to set at liberty those who are captive.

Christ also instructed his church to make disciples. This means leading people to make professions of faith in Jesus Christ as their personal Savior, and fully discipling them in the Christian faith so that they, too, can be people who go, minister, and teach others to observe all things in his name.

The mission pastor must believe fully, strongly, and completely in the work of the ministry, the work he has been commissioned and set aside to do.

He also must believe in the church. That seems a simple statement, but some young ministers do not believe in the institutional church. If he is to be effective, the mission pastor must accept the validity of the church; he must believe in the institution, in its essential nature. He must believe that it is truly Christ's church. The mission pastor must believe that Jesus loved the church and gave himself for it.

A person who does not believe in the church cannot start and develop a congregation into the fullness Christ intends. His lack of belief will always be a hampering influence, dividing his attention and splintering his efforts. A person cannot build what he does not believe in. The mission pastor, to serve effectively, must believe with all his heart that the church is the primary vehicle that Christ has chosen to be his messenger to the world. That belief should be second nature, worked through long before the minister ever arrives on the field.

The mission pastor also must see a need for the particular church he serves. If he questions the existence of that church and the need for it, it is not likely he will lead the church to be a growing, vibrant, effective congregation.

Two words characterize the mission pastor as he goes to serve on the field. One is calling. He must be aware of his calling to the ministry, to new church development, and to the specific church he will serve. The other is need. He must sense the need of the community—of those who are unchurched, unenlisted, and need ministry—and he must be aware that the church is the vehicle Christ has commissioned to meet that need in that specific place.

The Pastor's Spiritual Life

Don Flood was fond of saying such things as "Praise the Lord," and talking about how wonderful God is. He liked to tell his congregation about the glories of the "Spirit-filled life" and how much he enjoyed just walking and talking with Jesus.

But Don Flood was a sham. "Praise the Lord" was a catch phrase, a hollow echo which practically meant nothing to him. He knew that God is wonderful, but his life reflected little of the wonder. He knew about the Spirit-filled life, but the Holy Spirit was relegated to a back room of his life. He didn't walk and talk with Jesus; in fact, he seldom prayed anymore.

The words were coverups to hide a serious lack in Don Flood's life. Most of his spiritual life had drained away, leaving only pious-sounding words and nonpracticed truths in its place.

Don Flood had been so busy worrying about the spiritual needs of his congregation that he had neglected his own spiritual life. He had been so busy preaching and going that he forgot that he needed nurture, too.

Because he neglected his own spiritual needs, Don Flood became a cymbal chorus rather than a vibrant, spiritual man of God so needed in the small church of which he was pastor.

The mission pastor leading a weak, struggling mission congregation needs to be a vibrant, radiant spiritual person. His spirituality must be real, spurting from the wellspring of God's presence in his life. He cannot cover this lack with false piosity and dripping pious phraseology. This is a front, and most false fronts usually fall.

The mission pastor must take his cue from the people in the early days of Christianity. It was apparent that the leaders and preachers were spiritual men. Their lives, their ministry, their messages reflected that they had been with Jesus and took knowledge from him.

The effective mission pastor, in leading a mission congregation, can give a spiritual dynamic to the entire church, even though the facilities are makeshift, the finances are inadequate, the music is woefully lacking. If he radiates a spiritual dynamic—drawn from his own personal, close relationship with God—he can make worship and study meaningful experiences to all who come.

To be effective, the mission pastor must have a working relationship with the Holy Spirit. There are theological controversies raging throughout Christendom today about whether a person needs to be "filled with the Spirit," whether he needs "renewal," whether he needs the "baptism of the Holy Ghost," or a "deeper life" experience. It is not within the scope of this book to enter this theological controversy about the terminology one should use in achieving a close, current, full fellowship with the Holy Spirit. But it is absolutely essential for the mission pastor to have worked out in his own life the means whereby he is possessed by the Holy Spirit. He cannot effectively lead a congregation to grow into a stable, effective church unless he has, himself, been completely possessed by God's spirit.

Periodically, the mission pastor must experience personal cleaning. One of the things which can be very effective is a very simple, childlike routine of going off into a quiet place and making a list of the sins in his life. Then, he should pray and ask God to remind him of sins he may have forgotten, honestly and seriously seeking every nook and corner of his being for every sin of thought, word, deed, action, inaction, or whatever, putting them on his list.

Then, confession should be made, asking God's forgiveness as each sin is confessed. This procedure is like a bucket of rocks. If the bucket is filled with water, the amount of water it will hold is limited by the number of rocks. As a rock is removed, more water can be held by the bucket. So it is with our lives. Each time we remove a specific sin, we leave additional space for the Holy Spirit to dwell in greater fullness.

A simple anagram for prayer is the word *A C T S*. The four letters symbolize the aspects of prayer. *A* stands for adoration, as we adore God and come to love him more deeply. *C* stands for confession, as we lay our sin before God and confess him as our Lord. *T* stands for thanksgiving, as we give thanks to God for all things, both good and bad in our lives. *S* stands for supplication, as we speak humbly and contritely of our needs and the needs of others.

Prayer is an essential ingredient in the mission pastor's life. Without it, he will lose his spiritual strength. Spiritual life needs constant refreshing through constant contact with God.

Another element of spiritual life is personal devotions. The mission pastor must give time to his own devotions. In spite of all the pious platitudes and pulpit pronouncements that many preachers make, they would have to admit that private devotions is a neglected aspect of their own lives. These private devotions allow the mission pastor to find what God is saying to him. They are vastly different from and totally apart from sermon preparation.

The effective mission pastor must have a stated time for these devotions. If he does not have a regular time, the odds are he will not have any private devotions. He needs to establish a time, and to guard it as he guards other important times in his life. He should establish a plan, including both Bible reading and prayer. Many good plans exist, or a creative person can create his own plan. Whatever method is used, the private devotions need to be at a regular time and have a definite plan.

The pastor must exercise great personal discipline to hold to the routine and plan of his devotions. He must deal firmly with interruptions, allowing only the highest priority crisis to interfere with this particular activity.

As a further note, it must be strongly emphasized that the pastor's spiritual life sets the temperature for the church. It is as he is renewed, refreshed, filled, and fired anew that his spiritual strength is built. The spiritual strength and power comes from a close walk with God and from the infilling of the Holy Spirit. He cannot minister more than he has; if he is weak spiritually—through neglect, carelessness, lack of discipline, or ignorance—the church will be weak spiritually.

His inward life is built and strengthened from this constant and close contact with God. The inward life will be reflected in the outward life. Jesus himself commented that it is from the "abundance of the heart the mouth speaketh." If the pastor is filled with love and joy and victory, he will reflect these values to those around him.

The mission pastor is the most visible expression of that congregation in the new community. He is generally the first acquaintance that most people have with the new church. He is the new church personified to most people. Therefore, his life needs to be above reproach.

His speech needs to be clean, kind, friendly. Failure to be friendly is inexcusable in any Christian, but is unforgiveable in a minister of the gospel. He must be kind and friendly in his speech, life, and manner if he is to adequately represent God and the congregation.

The mission pastor's conduct needs to be Christian and above reproach. He should be a person who pays his debts, is honest, and is straightforward in all things.

His ethical standards need to be thoroughly Christian. Basic to all these things—demeanor, speech, conduct, ethical standards is his thought. His mind must remain clean.

One of the greatest helps a pastor has in maintaining a vibrant spiritual life is fellowship with other good Christians. In the early days of the development of a mission congregation, fellowship of the members of the church may be very limited, and many of the people may be very new Christians who drain more than they give in spiritual strength. The mission pastor should seek fellowship with other pastors in the community. Even though there may be some theological disagreement, the mission pastor will find a great unity of spirit in the basic fellowship of people who accept Jesus Christ as Lord and Savior. Such contact will give spiritual strength and uplift to tho mission pastor.

The mission pastor also will find that there are great Christians in every community. There are lay people, sometimes elderly saints of the Lord, who give great strength and spiritual boost to the mission pastor.

Special opportunities for renewing Christian fellowship also are offered through retreats—which may be get-togethers of the pastor's own denomination or other denominations. Just getting away for a few days in the company of Christian brothers and sisters often gives a needed boost to allow the mission pastor to come back fresh and full of steam, ready to work.

The Mission Pastor and His Faith

Bill McDuffey was a graduate of an evangelical seminary who was called to pastor a mission congregation in Townville. The seminary was fundamental and evangelistic in its statement of faith, but questions of biblical faith were intruding into the curriculum.

When McDuffey arrived on the field, his theological foundations had been established. He did not believe in the Genesis account of creation, believing it was merely a clip-and-paste job of editors who assembled the Bible. Other aspects he considered historic clap-trap, including the flood account and the Jonah story.

Bill also did not believe in the virgin birth, noting that "it was not important how he came, just that he did." To him, Jesus was a philosopher, a radical social reformer and a good man. Bill steered away from preaching or teaching about the blood atonement because he really didn't believe such a thing was necessary.

For the young man, Paul was a sexist, a racist, and many of the things the apostle wrote had to be interpreted in their context and were not really applicable to modern life.

McDuffey didn't really believe in the church as an evangelical instrument but thought it was more a base from which to minister in the community. Ministries should be designed to develop the people as fully as possible, but should not seek to get them to change their own religious or traditional beliefs he explained.

New Hope Mission did not grow. Bill didn't see the use or the place of the church, so, to him, it didn't make much difference.

The mission pastor who has no faith cannot lead people to a knowledge of faith in Christ. The mission pastor must have a fundamental faith and belief in Jesus Christ and in the essential elements of Christianity before he can lead in a faith-sharing operation.

The mission pastor must believe in the basics of Christianity. There are many areas of the Christian faith where Christians differ between denominations—and even within denominations—about the theological aspects. But the core fundamentals of the Christian faith are the basics: that man is separated from God by sin, brought into the world by Adam. God, loving his creation, sent Jesus Christ into the world to live, die, and be resurrected to bond that breach between God and man. Any pastor who has serious doubts about the basic core of the Christian faith—the heart of the gospel—is not likely to ever grow a church.

The new birth is one of the basics of Christianity. The new birth is a fundamental doctrine of evangelical Christianity. It holds that when a person professes faith in Jesus Christ, he is born again into the family of God. The firm belief in this on the part of the mission pastor is essential if he would develop a new congregation.

New congregations basically grow from new converts and not from transfer growth. If the congregation does grow primarily from transfer growth, its reason for being is extremely doubtful and the validity of its existence is quite questionable. It is from people who have been born again through belief in Jesus Christ that new congregations are built.

The Bible, as the Word of God, is an essential element of faith of the mission pastor. One of the basic foundations of church planting is that the "Bible is foundational to church planting." The Bible contains the pattern for church planting; the Bible is the basis for the existence of the church; and the Bible is a basic tool for the church planter.

If the mission pastor would be an effective church planter and developer of a new congregation, he must believe that the Bible is the Word of God, and he must use it as his essential tool in reaching people for Jesus Christ and for church membership.

The lostness of man is another fundamental doctrine of the Christian faith that the mission pastor must accept. If he does not believe that unchurched people are genuinely lost without Jesus Christ and doesn't firmly believe that Christ is the way, the truth, and the life, he will not develop a mission congregation. He must be a man possessed and driven by the realization of what humanity's lostness means.

Christ as Savior and Lord is perhaps the most overarching statement of the Christian faith that must be accepted by the mission pastor. If he does not see Christ as totally unique, as the Son of God, he does not possess the basic ingredient of Christianity. The mission pastor must see Christ as Savior and Lord, as *his* Savior and Lord, and as the one who needs to be Savior and Lord of all mankind. If he does not see Christ in this way, he cannot effectively lead a mission congregation to grow and reach people.

The role of the church is a fundamental element in the basic faith of the mission pastor. He must see the church as having an essential role in evangelizing and discipling his community. He must see the church as the institution Christ has selected to work through. If he does not see the church in this manner, he cannot lead in growth and development of the local congregation.

The Mission Pastor and People

Mel Adams was having trouble with the deacons at Northridge Church in Plainsville. For the most part, the deacons were a group of older men who held fast to the philosophy: "We have always done it this way and we will never change."

Adams had been frustrated in a number of efforts to increase the outreach and ministry of the church during the three years he had served Northridge.

He had attempted to establish a church council, and a church missions committee, but the "board" of deacons had torpedoed the ideas. He wanted to change the church training structure to add new, learning experiences, but the "board" shot that idea down, too. Soon, the deacons meetings became armed camps, with each side distrusting the other. Gossip and rumors came out of the deacon body, aimed at Mel and his ministry.

Mel, whose livelihood was tied to the church, as was the security of his wife and three children, was very upset by the turn of events. Never before had Mel been confronted by a group of people who neither respected, loved, nor followed him.

Mel began to pray. After some pouring out of his bitterness and frustration, he began to ask God to give him the power to love the deacons, particularly one individual who seemed bent on thwarting every effort the pastor made.

As Mel prayed, he felt a change in his own heart. Gradually, the bitterness and frustration left. "I really can love those guys, no matter what they do to me," he told his wife. A few weeks later, he was able to say, without modification, "I love those guys."

Mel Adams had found that, from his point at least, he should live the scriptural admonition: "By this shall all men know that ye are my disciples, if ye have love to one another" (John 13:35).

The mission pastor must have genuine love for people. Without love, he cannot be an effective leader. Without love, he cannot reach people. Without love, he cannot minister in Jesus' name. Without love, he cannot be God's man, leading, preaching, teaching, and ministering in the mission congregation.

He must be a person with compassion for the people. He must hurt when they hurt, grieve when they grieve. He must have empathy for those whom he would serve.

The mission pastor must be a person who has goodwill toward all men. He must not carry a chip on his shoulder but must desire good for all. He must not rejoice at ill luck, but must wish and hope and seek the best for all people.

He must be concerned about other people; concerned about their problems, their needs, their burdens, their sorrows. He must—to use the old-fashioned word—be burdened for people, feeling a crushing load of concern for the people of the community who are unchurched, unenlisted, who hurt, who have problems or sorrows. He must feel that the Christ he serves has something to offer to the people.

He must love people so that their lostness is a matter of very personal grief to him. He must love people of all classes, whether garbage men or bank presidents, fifth-grade dropouts or persons with advanced degrees. He must love people of all cultures, all races, all nationalities. He must not draw back from any person because of smell, color, or other element.

He must love people and be people conscious. Many ministers are real estate oriented or program oriented or building oriented or finance oriented. Many pastors are happy piddling with records, making marks on paper. But to be effective, the mission pastor must mix and mingle, tough and love, minister and care. He must love people and want to be with them.

The Mission Pastor and His Attitudes

The mission pastor, if he would serve effectively, must have the mind of Christ. He must seek to grow to the point where he can fulfill the biblical injunction: "Let this mind be in you, which was also in Christ Jesus." He must earnestly and prayerfully seek to let his mind be the mind of Christ.

If he seeks it, the fruits of the Spirit—mentioned in Galatians 5:22-23—would come alive in his personal life.

If he seeks the mind of Christ, he will be a person in whom love will be evident. He will be a person in whom joy will show, as opposed to sorrow and depression.

He will be a person who is peaceable as opposed to the irritable, fractious spirit of the world. He will be a person who is long-suffering rather than having a chip on his shoulder. He will be a person who is gentle and kind, as opposed to gruff and rude.

He will be a good person, with all that implies in spiritual cleanliness and morality, as opposed to the unclean, filthy person of the world.

He will be a person of faith who believes that God *is* and God *does*, and God *will*, and God *can*.

He will be a person who is generous in giving of self. He will be a humble person, seeking to do the work of Christ because he has the mind of Christ.

He will not be proud and egotistical, but humble and loving. His goals are spiritual goals, not material ones. Serving in a mission congregation is no place to be and yearn for the fleshpots of the world. Holding on to materialism while seeking spiritual aims falls into the category of wanting God and mammon.

If he is seeking the mind of Christ, the mission pastor will reflect in his own life those values which will stand the test of time.

15. Important Relationships for the Mission Pastor

Marvin Whiteside answered the telephone in the office of the Jefferson association of churches. The call had broken his concentration on answering the mail, but the message Roy Curtis gave him disturbed him deeply.

"I felt you should be the first to know," Curtis began. "My wife and I have separated. She has taken up with another man. I don't know what I'll do."

Curtis was pastor of a growing congregation—Lincoln Avenue Church—and seemed to have everything going his way. He had been a hard-working pastor, active in associational life, and once serving on one of his denomination's state committees.

There was a long pause on the telephone. Whiteside sat silent, stunned by the news.

Finally, Curtis broke the silence: "I admit I've been so busy the past few years doing the Lord's work that I forgot my own family. I created my own problem. She never would have done this if I hadn't ignored her so much."

Curtis went on to tell how his wife had become increasingly belligerent about his church work, forcing herself to be polite and correct when around church members but cold and hostile when at home.

She had taken their three children with her when she left. They, too, had scars from the pressures of the pastorate and the general lack of fatherly concern.

"Pray for us . . . Pray for us," Curtis told Whiteside. "It's just so awful. . . ."

The mission pastor has a number of important relationships to which he must devote attention. First and foremost is his role as husband and father. Then he must give attention to his relationships with the church and its members, with the community, and with

124   PLANTING NEW CHURCHES

his denomination. If he fails to pay attention to any of these areas,
he runs the danger of overbalancing his life.

The primary relationship which must be nurtured and attended
is that of his relations with his family. Pastoring a mission congregation often is a lonely assignment. Frequently, the pastor serves in
an area where his own denomination is weak, so mutual fellowship
with the other pastors of his faith in the area is limited and infre-
quent. Often he is far removed from family and friends. It is a
lonely work, and the loneliness of the work is shared by the pastor's
wife.

Many mission pastors moving to a new and strange area experience culture shock. The wife also experiences the strangeness and
loneliness of the new area and the cultural assault. The couple discover the local people know absolutely nothing about the denomination or, if they do, have stereotyped misconceptions that are shock-
ing to a newcomer's family. One Southern pastor recently moved
to a community in North Dakota and found that most of the residents
of the town thought his denomination was a very peculiar group,
in fact, some thought they were "snake handlers" or some such
thing.

When the pastor moves from an established, strong First-church
situation where he is accepted as a leader and given respect, where
his wife is treated as "first lady," and goes to a small, unknown
community, the family suffers the pains of relocation.

The pastor should devote attention to his wife, making sure she
is an integral part of the ministry. He should help her to have whatever part in the work she desires and should help her adjust to
the new situation.

The pastor also should seek to provide his wife with spiritual
growth opportunities and should pray regularly and frequently with
her. In their personal life, attention should be given a high priority,
or the pastor and his wife will grow apart and become isolated from
each other.

One of the first ministries a pastor has is to his family. He must
work diligently and assign time to his own family unit.

Often, mission congregations have makeshift facilities, limited lay
leadership, and an irregular age span of children. As a result, many
children's activities are lumped together, without the close age grad-
ing of a larger church. Pastor's families must be prepared for this.

The pastor must seek to enhance the spiritual life of his own family, and should carefully explain the reason as far as the nature of the ministry. This is particularly true of teenagers.

An Example: Norman Hill recently moved his wife and two teenage children to Cedarville, a community of 15,000 in a growing area. There were no churches of his denomination within 100 miles and 65 percent of the people who lived in the city and its county were unchurched.

Hill's sixteen-year-old daughter, Tricia, experienced severe loneliness in moving from the school where she had spent six years. She moved to a school where she knew no one and where she was not involved in any activities. The Hills' son, Joe, readily accepted the outdoors nature of the new community and enjoyed skiing, snowmobiling, snowshoeing, and all the other winter sports. But Tricia had a hard time.

Among her problems was the fact that she had moved from an active youth group of some twenty young people to a church situation in which she and Joe were the only teenagers.

Hill set a priority to spend time with his family and particularly with Tricia. He patiently talked to her about his sense of call to the church and the need for the new mission. He could not take away the pain entirely, but his presence and concern helped to ease the hurt.

Mission pastors often face budgetary limitations. They must learn to squeeze each nickel until the buffalo bellows. New churches often must live for several years before maturing and growing to the point of financial stability. Most major denominations have salary subsidies for pastors in new church development, but, necessarily, these funds must phase out after the first three to five years. The church seldom lavishes a tremendous salary on the mission pastor. Because of financial limitations, the mission pastor must learn to budget carefully and must adopt good management practices. If he does not, he runs the risk of becoming insolvent and thus damaging the name and reputation of the denomination, the church, and Christianity in the town.

Mission pastors must also be aware that the pastor is the single-staff person in the church. There is no secretary, no janitor, no educational help, no yardman, no music help. The pastor is IT. As a result, he often finds himself siphoning off his time doing the "monkey

work" of janitor, yardman, plumber, secretary, editor of the church
newsletter, and sometimes even director of music. A creative pastor
will soon find volunteers to help with all these things, but the unusual
demands of being the only paid staff member of a church often
place great pressure on the mission pastor and his time.

The mission pastor also frequently has an urgency for the church
to grow. He faces pressures of financial phaseout, monetary contribution by church members, attitude, denominational expectation,
the desire of the people to expand, and a whole psychological pano-
ply of pressures. All of these combine to give him a compelling
feeling that he must be busy every minute of every day, leaving
little or no time for his family.

The mission pastor must be aware of the situation which faces
him in a small, lonely situation. He must have his eyes open and
be aware of the things he will face. Prior planning often eliminates
unpleasant surprises and shattered hopes, disrupted family life and
financial problems.

The mission pastor can plan positively to deal with these items.
Armed with the good experiences of some fellow mission pastors
and forewarned by the bad experiences, the mission pastor should
be motivated to make some positive plans for good family relationships. If he has faced up to his situation—recognizing that it is lonely
for his family as well as for him, that they have had a culture shock,
that the program for children is inadequate, that finances are tight,
that one man can't do everything, and that growing should not
take precedence over his family—he should be ready to do some
positive planning to safeguard his own family relationships.

Make the most of the time available to spend with the family.
If time is limited, the mission pastor should be aware of how precious
the time he actually has can be. If he can give each child fifteen
minutes of undivided attention each day, he will make great strides
in understanding. The mission pastor also should be a careful listener
to his wife and children at mealtimes. Listening will do a great
deal of good. The mission pastor should not waste time; he should
make the most of the time he has.

Plan regular time with the family. The mission pastor should
plan a day off each week, let the church know what day that is,
and hold rigidly to it. Pastors are frequently the worst abusers of
God's command that man should work six days and rest one. Most

pastors seem to think the church—and God—can't get along without them. One large new church grew from scratch to 2,000 members in seven years. The pastor and staff (educational director and music minister) prayerfully reviewed their family responsibilities and came up with the idea that their priorities should be: First, God; second, family; third, church. As they try to hold to this concept, they have found they do a better job in their church work as well as in their family life.

Include some recreation. "All work and no play makes Jack a dull boy," says the old proverb. The workaholic who never gets his mind off the nitty-gritty of the work will never be totally effective in growing a church. The pastor needs some recreational activity. He needs to relax without feeling guilty. He needs to inject fun into the seriousness of the work. The pastor and his family need to include some recreational activity in their family planning. If he can include recreation along with quality family time, he has killed two birds with one stone. The pastor will be appreciated more by his family and his people if he can discipline himself to provide some recreation for himself and his family. He also needs to remember that even computers need downtime, and that if he takes time to relax and be refreshed, he will be more effective and energetic in what he does.

Maintain family devotions. One of the foundations of church planting is that the "Holy Spirit is basic to all that is done in church planting." If the mission pastor and his family fail to include family devotions in their daily agenda, they can short-circuit the Holy Spirit's operation in the entire endeavor. Family devotions will do much to relax the tension of the overtaxed schedules of the whole family team and rejuvenate their spirits as well. Further, the pastor should emphasize the place and necessity of family devotions to his congregation. The pastor's family should set the example, showing the effectiveness and the essential nature of family devotions.

There are numerous good examples and bad examples of pastors who neglect or enhance family relationships. Recently, in a missions conference attended by 100 pastors, the emphasis was on soul-searching for sin problems. The pastors were asked to make recommitment, and some fifteen pastors—15 percent of the group—in private conversations, admitted to deep-seated family problems which needed solution. One pastor revealed that his teen-age daugh-

ter had been involved with drugs, prostitution, and had an illegiti-
mate child.

At the same conference, several pastors admitted to intense frustration with the pastoral ministry due to relationship problems with
lay leadership and church members in general.

On the other hand, some of the pastors noted extreme satisfaction
with their lives and their ministry. One pastor has two sons, both
of whom are in the Christian ministry. Another has two children,
a boy and a girl, who both are in college preparing for church-
related work.

The mission pastor, or any other pastor for that matter, can prevent unhappy surprises if he will carefully nurture and cherish his
family. The family is a crucial unit, one which the mission pastor
must care for physically and spiritually.

Church Relationships

*Morris Clifton was still a young man—twenty-nine—when he
was called to be pastor of Spruce Baptist Church. He had come
from a smaller church which was growing, but when he moved to
the large, multibuilding plant of Spruce Church, he was somewhat
intimidated.*

*Like many young men, Clifton masked his insecurity with seem-
ing overconfidence. He wanted to give the impression that he knew
exactly what to do in every situation. He could diagnose immediately
the ills of the church and give a simple solution to a complex
problem.*

*Clifton, in short, attempted to become a dictator. He would come
to business meetings and introduce new items of business neither
the church council nor the deacons had heard about.*

*He forced a few issues in the early days of his ministry, but finally
several of the members got their dander up. They had a private
session with Clifton and told him, among other things, that he
was not being quite honest with either himself or them, that he
was trying to make every decision and rule every issue, and that
he was ruining the fellowship of the church.*

*Morris listened diligently, but his pride was hurt. He complained
to his wife that the church didn't appreciate him and started getting
his friends to suggest his name to other prestigious churches. Morris's
ego wouldn't let him correct a situation his pride had caused.*

Because of his dictatorial attempt, he damaged the fellowship of the church and made the ministry harder for the man who succeeded him.

The mission pastor needs to cultivate his relations with his church and its members. He should work closely with the members and with the leadership, exhibiting honesty, character, ethical behavior, and love in all that he does.

When he is relating to the church, the pastor should do all that he does in love. If he does not love his people, he cannot serve them well. If he does not love them, he should ask God to give him that gift, so that he can be God's man in that place.

There are several key elements to a pastor's relationship with his people.

Honesty.—The mission pastor should have an honest, straightforward relationship with his people. He should keep them informed as to his activities. Everything should be up front between the pastor and the people. People will follow a pastor who is working and setting an example in well-disciplined Christian living and serving.

Lay involvement.—The mission pastor should make every provision possible to involve the laypeople in the ministry, outreach, and work of the church. He can use people in many jobs. He can delegate responsibility. He can lighten the load on himself by getting other people to help. Even if he does not have a staff, he can free himself for higher priority tasks—witnessing and preparation to preach—by delegating responsibilities and using volunteers. A word of caution. The pastor cannot give work assignments to lay persons and then dawdle. If he does so, his efforts too will boomerang.

Loving fellowship.—Loving fellowship ought to characterize the relations of the pastor and the people. He must love his people sincerely and have a warm, close, personal relationship with them. Developing a new church is wearing and tearing on the laity as well as on the pastor. All of the people—pastor and lay persons—need to know they are loved and appreciated. Then they will work all the harder.

Visitation of members.—Many young pastors are confused over whether they should visit just the unchurched and sick or whether they should visit their own members as well. In new work, priority must be given to intensive visitation of prospects for the new church, but some regular cycle of visitation of members of the church is essential if a warm relationship is to be developed and maintained. Members—particularly problem members—should not be allowed to absorb too much of the pastor's time, but he should devote some time and effort to cultivating the members, getting to know them, building a respect level, and developing the warm relationship so badly needed in churches.

The mission pastor also should develop warm, close, considerate relationships with the leadership of the church. As a new congregation grows, lay leadership is reached and developed. The church will then have deacons, church council members, or other key leaders. The pastor should work and plan closely with these persons if his leadership is to have maximum effectiveness. The mission pastor should not bypass these leaders in the decision making or promotional processes. When support for a certain project or course of action is diversified throughout the leadership group, there are more persons promoting that activity, and its chances of acceptance by the church body as a whole are enhanced.

One of the foundation blocks of church planting is that "participation planning at all levels is essential for effective church planting." This principle continues into the growth and development phases of the new congregation.

Community Relationships

John Forsythe was called to a small, five-family mission congregation in Chaparral. The small mission congregation had been struggling for three years to stay alive. The community scarcely knew the church existed. It certainly had made no impact on the community.

After arriving in Chaparral, Forsythe visited pastors of the other denominations, establishing a friendly, noncompetitive relationship, explaining who he was and what he believed and that he was seeking to reach people for Jesus Christ.

Several of the pastors shared names of prospects for the church. Others openly welcomed him because he represented a different theological stance and would attract a different group of people. Some, of course, were reserved. Toward them, Forsythe maintained a warm, open, friendly demeanor.

The pastor participated in the ministerial association and in community and civic events. He visited the religion writer at the daily newspaper and, after several episodes of coffee and conversation, Forsythe established a warm friendship. He did not manipulate that friendship, but found the writer was receptive to articles and announcements about church activities.

In similar fashion, Forsythe visited city hall and established personal relationships with leaders there. He came to know and have the trust of the hospital administrator, the welfare-agency people, the school administrator, several doctors, dentists, a lawyer, the leading banker, and officials at the city and county jail.

As the months progressed, Forsythe and his church had increasing visibility and credibility in Chaparral. Many of the people with whom Forsythe had made friends were in positions to offer valuable counsel or aid as the church grew and prospered.

The new congregation must be seen as an integral part of the community; it must not be an interloper, a stranger, invader, or parasite. The church and its pastor must inject themselves fully and completely into the life and activities of the city. The congregation can never be an organization which exists for its own selfish interests.

Since the pastor is the most visible expression of the new church, his personal involvement and relationships in the community become most important. As he is active in community matters, he must retain one of the basic foundations of church planting: "We must retain and maintain the redemptive note in all that we do." In his involvement, he makes friends who need the gospel of Jesus Christ. As he is involved, he will find natural opportunities for witnessing. He should take these opportunities as they occur.

Relationships with other religious groups.—A spiritual support system often is found between pastors of different denominations as they come to know each other. Such contact offers pastors of different traditions an opportunity to become friends, to bolster each other, and to encourage each other. Every religious tradition also has unusual ability to communicate to various segments of society and to people of different mind-sets. A mutual sharing of prospects and contacts often occurs when pastors become good personal friends.

The ministerial association is a good place to come to know fellow pastors in the community. In addition to fellowship, friendship, and sharing, this group also provides continuing educational opportunities to keep the pastors from growing rusty. Community and moral issues often are discussed and action organized in these bodies. High-attendance day often is promoted jointly through this group. In some cases they participate in joint publicity, cooperative advertising at the entrance to the city, in the Yellow Pages, radio stations, and in the newspaper.

The mission pastor also may want to make contact with the local council of churches. Research data often is available, and membership is not necessary to share in the benefits of such groups. However, a financial contribution to cover the cost of the data would be a courteous thing to do.

Relationships with government offices and leadership.—Sometimes small church groups sit back and criticize government operations, making no effort to get acquainted, to work for betterment, or to register their feelings. Some have formed preconceived notions of what they can and cannot do and of what can and cannot be done in a community. Many simply assume they may not do such things as door-to-door visitation and thereby sit back and do nothing. In many communities, a permit is required but can be secured without problem. This is illustrative of the things which might occur.

The size and structure of the community will dictate the relationships most important to the mission operation. Mention has already been made of city and county planning commissions. The mission pastor should become acquainted with the mayor, the city manager, councilmen and women, and office personnel. The same is true of the county sheriff and other law enforcement officers. Key school administrators in the community are important contacts and may open significant doors in the day-to-day work with the youth in the area.

The mission pastor also should have a working knowledge of the operations of government, who to contact, what forms to fill out, which office to go to. This knowledge may save many unnecessary steps. Knowledgeable persons in city and county governments often are helpful in teaching the mission pastor the ropes of county or city government.

Relationships with civic groups.—The pastor of a mission congregation simply doesn't have time to be a joiner of many organizations. However, he should be friendly with these civic groups—Parent-Teacher Associations, YMCA/YWCA, Kiwanis, Rotary, Lions, and other organizations such as the Chamber of Commerce and Development. He should respond to invitations for invocations and appearances on programs. Contacts with these groups could prove very helpful when the mission pastor needs support of key leadership in a community. Many times those who are most civic minded and thus open to new churches are members of these organizations.

The mission pastor should not remain aloof from these groups. He is now a resident of the community and should inject himself as completely as possible in them. Remaining aloof is one of the reasons Christianity and the church's voice often is not heard in the halls of government, the civic organizations, and the community-betterment groups. The pastor should seek to make his voice heard and his influence felt in every way possible.

Relationships with the media.—Cultivation of the personnel involved in the media—radio, television, and newspapers—is an essential part of the work of the mission pastor. Cultivation of religion editors, station managers, and newsmen is desirable when done tactfully. However, such cultivation should not be done with an intent to manipulate but only with the motive to establish mutually fruitful relationships. The use of news articles can be even more valuable than can advertisements, and frequently the editor or religion writer is happy to publish such articles.

Personnel who work with radio and television should also be cultivated. The national radio-television office of the denomination often has public service programs of high quality. Often all it takes is an indication of interest on the part of a local group to get the programs on the air. Audition tapes can be obtained to demonstrate the quality and content of the programs to the station management. Such broadcasts will help to establish the reputation and credibility of the mission congregation. Well prepared, high quality broadcasts done by professionals will do more to help the struggling congregation than will an ego-building broadcast where the preacher or congregation attempt to do what they cannot do well.

Relationships with business people.—Lawyers, real estate brokers, bankers, professionals of all categories should be cultivated. Frequently, the educational level and expertise of such persons intimidate struggling congregations with the results that these people are not cultivated. Many of the people in this category often are ignored by evangelicals in day-to-day visitation and cultivative activities. Church people—and especially pastors—need to be aware that these people are in need of witness and cultivation as much as anyone else.

The business and professional people often have busy schedules, and the pastor should not impose on them. However, through using some creativity, he can make opportunities for brief visits, a cup of coffee, or a luncheon. Cultivation of one lawyer may open the door to several others; the same approach will work with other professions, as well

Denominational Relationships

Mountainview Association was a small group of churches in a pioneer area. Each of the sixteen churches affiliated was struggling, and none had large memberships.

But, through the efforts of Director of Missions Ralph Wood, there was a warm fellowship among the churches. He encouraged the pastors to see each other socially and often organized a Ping-Pong tournament for the pastors to get together and share problems.

There was an air of celebration and victory—sort of like a big, family reunion—when the association held its monthly meetings. Most of the sessions were preceded by a covered-dish supper, and representatives from each of the churches were on hand, even though some had to travel many miles to attend.

Pastor's conferences were not just business meetings but were times of spiritual renewal. Through the newly encountered relationships, the pastors and people of Mountainview Association were strengthened and encouraged to return to their fields.

The association also provided counseling services as well as materials for many programs. Wood, a pastor of vast experience before moving into the administrative role, was a "pastor's pastor" and often encouraged the young men who were serving the churches of the association.

Because Wood and the others of the association cared, the denominational relationship established in the sixteen struggling congregations was a bond of love and strength.

The mission pastor, serving in lonely and often depressing situations, needs friends. Often, pastors of his denomination who serve neighboring churches can become close friends and a source of spiritual strength. The knowledge that the pastor isn't an Elijah—the only one serving the Lord—is helpful and can often stave off depression and despair.

Church members, also, can benefit from close contact with sister churches. Exchange visits, special events, joint meetings of fellowship nature can help develop solidarity of the denominational fellowship.

The district association of churches is important to the ministry of the mission pastor and to the development of the congregation. Through meetings on a district level, the people can be given specialized training, helping them learn more effectively. At the same time, they learn that Christianity is more than just the one, small band of believers but is a much larger fellowship of Christians. The district meetings also can serve to encourage and revive the congregation through fellowship, celebration, and personal contact.

The whole purpose of the new church becomes clearer in the minds of the congregation as they come to understand local, district, state, national, and world-mission programs of work. The knowledge that they are part of something great—something God has established—can be a great experience for the members of the congregation.

The director of associational missions for the local association is ideally situated to be a pastor's pastor, giving counsel and help where needed. Mission pastors frequently overlook this function of the director of missions and therefore miss a great blessing. The director of missions also can open doors by providing sources of assistance for almost any need which arises in the church.

The state denominational office has resources to help the mission pastor and congregation by providing funds and opportunities for growth and development. Normally, there are several staff persons who specialize in religious education and can help the mission pastor devise programs of training and teaching for the small, local congregation. Evangelism specialists can give training and assistance in developing the congregation into a body of witnesses. Stewardship development, missionary education, youth work, public relations, ethnic missions, and many other areas of special attention are available from staff persons on the state level.

And often the state office can provide materials for use in the local congregations. And, importantly, often the material is free.

The state office is a source of friendly assistance and counsel in the growth and development of the local congregation.

National offices of the denomination normally work through state and regional offices but offer many resources to the mission congregation. The national office staff persons often are eager to help the struggling mission.

The mission congregation needs to be educated about the existence and purpose of the various agencies of the denomination. Such education is part of their Christian training and development. Later, when they become mature workers, they will know where to turn for assistance.

Many mission congregations—and established ones as well—exhibit an abysmal ignorance about the functioning of the denomination of which they are a part. There are many facets to most denominations, and many resources are available. Frequently, the excellently prepared materials and personnel go unused simply because of the ignorance of the mission pastor and the congregation.

The materials, personnel, and resources are there to be used. They were set aside for that purpose. Training opportunities will strengthen the congregation and its individual members. Resource materials can build awareness of special promotions or special needs.

As a new Christian worker, the mission pastor often will be delighted and amazed to get a glimpse of the larger fellowships of which he is a part.

16. Discipling and the Mission Pastor

"Go ye therefore into the whole world and make disciples . . ."
was one of Pastor Charles Germany's favorite verses. It was a
verse he wholeheartedly tried to apply as he served Hampton's
Trinity Church.

Germany was a middle-aged pastor. He had experience in an
established church and the Hampton congregation was the third
mission he had started and nurtured.

His philosophy was to win people to a faith in Jesus Christ
and then to train them in basic Bible doctrine so they could be
strong Christians. He also aimed at teaching them how to share
their faith effectively, winning other new converts to the church.

Germany believed one of his most effective tools at discipling
was through the pulpit ministry. He preached evangelistic sermons
each Sunday morning but gave Sunday night and Wednesday
night to teaching messages. He kept a close eye on the topics and
subject matters of the Sunday School and training-hour material,
trying to tie his messages in with what the church members had
learned, reinforcing their knowledge from the pulpit.

He firmly believed that the church should give birth to strong,
healthy "babes" and then grow them up systematically and
soundly.

The growth and development of a mission congregation is
achieved through reaching new believers in Christ, and then helping
them grow up in the Christian faith. Historically, we have called
this making disciples. The thrust is reaching people and then teaching them "to observe all things" as he commanded us.

There are many activities involved in the process of discipling
people. Visitation makes cultivative converts; preaching persuades
and teaches; evangelism converts; ministries make friends; outreach
programs touch lives; Bible teaching edifies; training helps in grow-

137

ing; missionary programs develop a missions conscience; stewardship enriches; and music celebrates.

All of these activities are part of the discipling process, and none should take precedence over any other. Each has its place, and each strengthens the whole program and process. The mission pastor must be constantly aware of his discipling role. He is not a one-dimensional character; he is multifaceted in his roles and responsibilities.

Visitation

Every visit the pastor makes may not be evangelistic, but if the persons are unchurched, it should have an evangelistic intent in which to sow seeds for a more direct witness later.

The visitation program must be systematic from start to finish, well organized, well operated, well checked. The records must be maintained accurately and in an organized fashion. The appointments must be made gracefully. The pastor or the people must be trained and able to follow the leading of the Holy Spirit in a visitation situation.

Also, the visitation program must be regular. It must have a cadence and a routine. Haphazard, on-again-off-again visitation programs will not grow a church. This is particularly applicable to the mission pastor, but also applies to the lay visitors as well.

Any pastor of a mission congregation must put a prospect file high on his priority list. He must have such a file. The file should be prepared from survey material discussed in earlier chapters, from community cultivation contacts, from visitors at services, from friends and neighbors or church members. Forms can be secured easily, and the mission pastor should select the form which is easiest for him to use. Multicarboned copies are helpful in maintaining files.

Likewise, pastors must maintain a church member visitation file, on which he records his visits and other material he finds helpful. By maintaining an orderly church-member visitation file, the pastor can systematically visit each member of the congregation in a reasonable period of time. New church membership rolls are not large, and a visit at least once a quarter is desirable. As the membership increases, the time schedule may need to be expanded. However, visitation of church members is an essential element in the growth of new Christians.

Every visit the pastor makes should have a spiritual impact. Because his time is precious, he should focus on the matters of highest interest. Talking about professional football, the weather, or fishing should not dominate the visit. These items can be used for conversation openers, but the conversation and the visit should center on spiritual matters.

Several methods may be used to help the pastor have a spiritual impact. He can discuss spiritual concerns (church membership, salvation); he can have prayer in the home before leaving; or he can leave a well-chosen piece of literature in the home that shows the name, address, telephone number of the new church.

The serious mission pastor should sincerely seek to make at least ten meaningful evangelistic visits per week, along with numerous cultivation visits that may be preliminary to the "net-drawing" visits. New churches are born of new Christians; new Christians are not born from osmosis but from direct evangelism with the gospel gladly and lovingly presented.

A mission pastor who makes less than ten evangelistic visits a week likely will not grow a church with any size or strength. Vigorous, aggressive, regular, systematic visitation is the key to building churches.

To make that many calls a week means the pastor must have a disciplined schedule. Time management will be very important. Several good works are available to help the pastor control his schedule.

One method which can save the pastor time is to adopt a visitation by appointment method. With the hectic life-style of many people, a more effective visit may be had by appointment at the convenience of the person to be visited. A volunteer in the new church with a good telephone voice can serve as a visitation-appointments secretary, calling and making appointments for the pastor to visit in homes.

Visitation, systematically and regularly, is essential to discipling new Christians. We must seek them out; they generally will not seek the church.

Preaching

Joe Mahoney was famed for his "Saturday Night Specials." Mahoney's specials weren't the cheap, small-caliber, generally unreliable pistols sold in pawn shops; his were the dull, uninteresting, small-

caliber, cheap sermons he put together late on Saturday night.

Mahoney was so busy during the week that he didn't have time to study and prepare for sermons.

Mahoney had not established priorities. One of the reasons was that he hated to read and boasted frequently that he didn't read a book a month, and that was only because he had to.

Because Mahoney's sermons were so deadly and dull, the worship service at the mission chapel was deadly and dull. There was no sense of celebration or worship; just a dead, innervating ennui.

Mahoney maintained a small congregation of faithfuls, and the people who visited did not return. They expected something more than they got from the messages and the service. Joe, because of his lack of priorities and habits, didn't deliver.

Preaching is the evangelical's primary contribution to main-line Christianity. Evangelicals believe in the preeminence of the pulpit in the worship service and church program. Preaching is central to our message and our method.

If the mission pastor becomes so busy he cannot effectively fill the role of preacher, he is failing to contribute the one dimension he needs to contribute to his particular community. There may be many other things being done in existing Protestant churches—well organized, well-staffed Sunday Schools, well-trained teachers, high-class music performed by professionals—but the pulpit ministry is the one thing which the new evangelical church has to offer. In many other churches, the emphasis is on the liturgy; in evangelical churches, the emphasis should be on the sermon. It is very important for the mission pastor to see and understand that one dimension he can bring to the community is an effective pulpit ministry.

The worship service is the focal point of all new mission services. Everything that is done in a mission congregation generally revolves around the worship services, because all other elements of the organization are weak, embryonic, or struggling to take form. The worship service is the one element which can be done in a creditable manner by a small group, and from it can come inspiration for all other parts of the church program.

The worship service—the pulpit ministry—sets the image of the new congregation. The building may be ugly or there may be no building at all. The church may not have a pipe organ or a robed choir. It may not even have adequate teachers or space for a church program. All of the elements probably will be incomplete to some degree. But the mission pastor, with his training, is the most complete of all the elements of the new church.

The mission pastor has training and possibly some experience. It is the mission pastor who can give an image of the new congregation to the community more completely than can any other part of the church program. How well the mission pastor does his job is going to establish the image of the church in the eyes of the community.

The pastor is usually the best prepared person in the church. He has the background, calling, experience, and training which is lacking in every other church member. The pastor also is the best prepared teacher and therefore needs to make the most of his opportunities to teach effectively. Teaching in Sunday School may be weak and dull. It may be ineffective or nearly nonexistent. Therefore, the pastor must compensate for the lack of adequate teaching by doing a good job of teaching through his sermons.

The mission pastor bears a heavy burden with his pastor-teacher gift and responsibility. If new converts and reclaimed Christians are going to be developed, the discipling process may have to be carried primarily by the pastor. The worship service may become the focus of the teaching/training ministry of the church.

There is a critical need to mold new Christians and to help them grow in matters of doctrine, stewardship, church polity, becoming workers, and becoming effective witnesses. This molding and development must largely take place in the pulpit ministry of the church.

If we have weak, milk-drinking Christians when we ought to have strong, meat-eaters, much of the blame must fall on the pastor. If Christians are to grow, he must bear a heavy share of the responsibility for that growth.

The worship service not only is the focus of the teaching ministry, it also is the focal point—the climax—of the entire week of community contacts through visits and publicity. Most visitors make their first visits to the worship service. Most form their opinion of the church, the pastor, the congregation, and Christianity as a whole through the worship service.

If the service is flat, dull, and boring, chances are the visitors— potential converts or reclaimed Christians—will not return. They have better things to do with their time than listen to a dull, flat sermon and lackadasical singing.

Since it is so critical, the mission pastor must carefully plan his sermons and prepare the worship services of which they will be an integral part. The services should be prayerfully organized. The service should contain all of the elements of worship: prayer, praise, dedication, and commitment. In selection of songs these elements should be expressed. Songs should not be picked by flipping through the hymnal five minutes before service time, but should receive attention. Much thought should be given to creating a worship service which is stimulating and joyous. The people should be participants. They have not come to watch a preacher perform, no matter how engaging he may be. They have come to take part and to experience the worship service through inclusion.

The worship service also should include reverential scripture reading, and people should get a sense of awe from being in God's house and listening to God's Word. But the reverence, dignity, and sense of awe should also be combined with genuine spiritual warmth.

Singing is an important part of the worship service, and nothing destroys a song service more than a deadpan song leader or an inadequate accompanist who continually hits sour notes on the piano or organ. There should be an adequate accompanist, even if the congregation has to scrape together money to hire one. An adequate accompanist is as crucial to the growth of a new congregation as is the presence of an effective preacher in the pulpit. Persons skilled in playing the piano or organ can lift a service into spiritual realms while persons unskilled can destroy even the efforts of the most brilliant preacher.

It may be that the pastor has the best voice in the congregation, and, if so, he should lead the music rather than let the song service deteriorate into a monotone, joyless struggling through hackneyed old hymns. When, however, a suitable music director can be found, the pastor should turn the responsibilities for leading the music over to him or her.

The mission pastor also should work toward the early development of a choir, even if it is only a quartet. In a very small congregation, a quartet or sextet can add attractiveness, warmth, spirit, and dignity to the worship service by singing prayer responses, calls to worship, and performing special music to serve as preparation for the sermon. Guest soloists also can enhance any worship service, adding spice, interest, and spirit.

The mission pastor also should pay careful attention to the place where the worship service will be held. Even if it is a storefront, it should be neat and clean. The meeting site should be made as attractive as possible, recognizing the limitations under which the pastor and congregation often work. Flowers—artificial or real— can be provided. Sometimes a simple hanging of a drape behind the pulpit, or the use of folding screens can aid in the spirit of worship. The sermon will be more effective if there are not distractions or things to attract the eye away from the minister. Nothing is more distracting, or discourging, than cobwebs in a conspicuous place or dust on the seats. People do not like to sit in dusty chairs. It doesn't take a lot of time and effort to make the meeting site clean, neat, and reasonably attractive.

There are three aspects to the sermon: planning, preparation, and delivery.

The plan should be based on the needs of people. If the pastor is actively involved in his community, he will know what the needs of the people are. He can then use this insight to prepare sermons which will relate to the people where they live and work.

Inasmuch as the pastor is involved in teaching as well as preaching, he might try preaching a series of sermons on relevant areas of need or do expository sermons on the books of the Bible. Sermons on relevant areas of need and what the Bible says about them, as well as expository sermons, are great aids in the teaching ministry.

The pastor also might want to prepare a brochure on a particular sermon or series of sermons. The brochure can serve as an introductory piece in visitation as well as communicating important information to prospects or unenlisted Christians. The brochure can be much more interesting and effective than a simple schedule of services.

The local newspaper also might be interested in printing news items about the sermon series in the religion section.

Many pastors who are involved with their communities do not lack for ideas for sermons. The idea comes easily; the preparation of the material and the organization of it into a sermon is the hardest part. Creative people often have a problem with following through on the actual preparation. The mission pastor must seek good ideas and then effectively carry through to make the ideas into good sermons.

In preparing to preach, the pastor should establish a study time and closely guard that time. It should be scheduled at a time he feels most inclined to study, whether morning, afternoon, or evening. The pastor, if he is to preach effective and interesting sermons, biblically based and spiritually motivating, must spend time in study. A good rule of thumb is three or four hours per day. The pastor's wife can be very helpful in guarding the study time, by answering telephone calls and in general shielding the minister while he studies.

Periodically, every minister should review sermon preparation texts studied in college or seminary. A rereading of the old texts could prove very helpful.

For the novice pastor who has not had the advantage of college or seminary and for the experienced pastor who has been out of school for some time, a sermon preparation book which would prove very helpful in review is *On the Preparation and Delivery of Sermons,* by John A. Broadus, revised by Jesse Burton Weatherspoon.

The mission pastor also would do well to invest in a good set of commentaries. He can do it one book at a time—making the expenditures as he preaches on the book of the Bible, or he can find a good sale and make a savings by purchasing an entire set at one time.

There are many good sermon preparation helps, expositions of books of the Bible, works on various topics, and often study guides. The effective pastor will look for such works and carefully study them.

Seminary library circulation services also are available for an annual fee. By subscribing to the service, the mission pastor can obtain any book in the library for a limited time. Such a service can be very helpful.

As the pastor prepares to preach, he also must keep in mind the needs, interests, educational level, and experiences of his people. He must relate the sermons to those things. A sermon with an illustration about plowing a field with a horse frequently doesn't mean very much to an inner-city or urban congregation where many of the members have never even seen a horse except of course, on television.

When the preacher has planned and prepared, it is time to deliver his sermon. He should check his content and delivery by listening to himself on recordings or having his family criticize his messages. If delivery is weak, the mission pastor should work to improve himself. Many opportunities offer themselves. He can take courses in speech at a nearby college or seminary. He can read books on the fundamentals of public speaking. He can simply get off by himself and practice, either in front of a mirror or with a tape recorder.

There is an urgency about the task of preaching. The competent mission pastor will realize the importance of the function and will set priorities and plans for his own development as he carries out the working of these gifts in his life and ministry.

Evangelism

Alfred Downs told his wife early one Sunday morning: "Boy, I'm going to blow them out of the tub today. I have a real evangelistic sermon. I'm going to preach on freedom in Christ, using Galatians 5:1."

Downs had prepared his sermon, checking with the commentaries and other expositions of Galatians on the topic of Christian freedom. He liked to preach and was an inventive and funny speaker.

But on that Sunday morning, he preached with fire and fervor about Christian freedom. But when the time for invitation came, he dwindled off and left the call to Christian commitment curiously nebulous and weak.

He stood at the front during the singing of "Just As I Am" and was secretly glad that no one came. He really didn't know what to do when someone responded to the invitation.

Downs wanted to be evangelistic, but he was afraid of and didn't know how to effectively handle people in the evangelistic services. Therefore, he shortened his arm and fell short of striking a full blow.

The effective mission pastor will have a carefully planned program of evangelism, for no mission can grow into a full church without making scores of new converts. It must be open, unapologetic, and done with full fervor. Churches are born out of new converts; churches which depend on transfer growth for their membership increase, generally have little excuse for their existence except as they evangelize the unchurched.

Evangelism must be carefully woven into the entire fabric of the church. Preaching, worship, education, visitation, ministry, training, outreach, Bible teaching, missionary education, stewardship development, and music ministry all must reflect an evangelistic aim.

Evengelism takes many forms. Mass evangelism varies in effectiveness from region to region across America, but such mass efforts must be a part of the evangelistic crusades or revivals. Many Christians will never be revitalized and renewed without periodic mass-evangelism efforts. Because mass evangelism is difficult, preparation must be carefully made with the best resource materials available. State and national evangelism offices have revival or crusade preparation plan books to assist the pastor with some good ideas, gleaned from experiences of many in successful crusades.

Personal evangelism, both on the part of the pastor and the people, is an imperative for the mission congregation. The pastor must not be afraid of direct confrontation evangelism. He must constantly remain sensitive to the spiritual needs of the unchurched, and be alert for every opportunity to witness.

Lay witness schools for training of the laity are imperative. The few lay people of a congregation, both young and adult, need to be sensitized and equipped to be regular, systematic witnesses. Some of the most successful mission pastors have found on-the-job training to be an effective method of training the laity in witnessing. Such training consists of the pastor taking the layperson with him as he makes evangelistic visits, showing by example, and then letting the layperson do the witnessing while the pastor is the silent partner. As lay witnesses are trained, they can then become trainers, working with new converts to train a second generation.

New converts often are eager to learn to share their newfound faith. The pastor who does not provide immediate opportunities often stifles the spiritual growth and stunts the Christian. Studies have proven that new converts often are more effective in winning others to Jesus Christ, because their enthusiasm is higher and their circle of friends is open to penetration.

The mission church should have a primary thrust of developing lay witnesses who are ready, eager, and capable of sharing their faith. Everyone should be involved in sharing his faith. This is the primary way by which a mission congregation will develop into a stable church.

Evangelistic preaching by the pastor is likewise a must. Evangelistic messages come alive when illustrations are used from current church visitation experiences. Because the pastor bears the burden for teaching his people, it is recognized that "teaching preaching" will be needed in the congregation. However, the morning service generally should be used as an evangelistic service. Visitors usually attend morning services, and more prospects are present. Therefore, the morning service should feature evangelistic preaching, coupled with a strong invitation to salvation, rededication, and church membership.

The evening services can be the service in which feeding of the sheep is accomplished. Generally evening services are attended by faithful Christians, thus offering an opportunity to teach through the sermon.

Pastors should work carefully on the art of giving an effective evangelistic invitation. Often the best evangelistic sermon is made ineffective because the invitation is bungled or the spirit of conviction is broken. The pastor who preaches evangelistic sermons and then flubs the invitation is doing only half a job. He must strongly draw the net, allowing God's Holy Spirit to use that time of conviction and commitment to the fullest.

Music is an effective evangelistic tool. Music seems to have a special ability to touch the hearts of people. One way in which music can be used effectively in evangelism is through use of visiting choirs. One church invited a visiting choir to give a nightly evangelistic music concert, interspersed with testimonies. After the concert, the pastor gave a short evangelistic message, followed by a strong invitation. In that particular church more than 125 persons were converted during the week.

Other possibilities include using guest soloists to present sermons in song for an entire worship service, with scripture and words of testimony woven through the carefully interrelated arrangement of songs.

Community Ministries

J. C. Houston was assigned to a dead church in Banning. The congregation dwindled when a nearby Air Force Base closed, and all of the members moved away.

Houston had the use of the whole church building, a rambling structure which adequately fitted the climate and culture of the area.

Houston began to cultivate the city and soon met Guy Marshall, director of welfare. During their conversation, Marshall told Hous-

ton that he had no place from which to distribute commodity food items to welfare recipients. Houston offered the use of the building, which he found was in the heart of the poverty pocket of Banning. Some 3,000 poverty-level families lived within a mile of the church.

The welfare distribution began, and, within a month, Houston had 3,000 persons coming through the church on distribution day. All he had to do was stand there and smile at them.

Houston met a young lawyer and enticed the attorney to offer free legal advice once a month. Likewise, he contacted two doctors and a dentist and set up a free medical clinic for the people who lived around the church.

He met a woman who had a counseling degree and encouraged her to offer counseling services through the church facilities. Houston set up a drug-abuse center, which the city fathers protested: "We don't have a drug problem here. All of our kids are good kids." But, in the first week of the drug-rap center, 240 kids showed up.

Houston also opened a clothing storehouse and a furniture depository in unused portions of the church. Within five months, he had more than twenty ministries operating from the old church building.

After the intensive period of ministry, Houston began worship services. On the inaugural day of services, more than 100 persons showed up. Because he had been sensitive to the needs of his community and the opportunities to serve, Houston nearly had an "instant church." It grew because of demonstrated love and care for the people of the community.

One of the foundation blocks of church planting is that we must build bridges to people. New mission congregations could be ministering congregations from the very beginning. The number and kind of projects may be limited by situations or resources, but ministries are imperative from the beginning. The group that proclaims "When we get big and strong, our buildings built, and we are self-supporting, we will minister" will be an introverted, self-centered church that looks to the community like a parasite which has come to take and not to give.

The new congregation needs to take a long, hard look at the needs and interests of the community and then to check availability and talents within its own numbers. After listing all possible ministries, priorities need to be established in keeping with degree of need or interest and the abilities of the group to respond to the needs. There must, however, be a balance between ministry projects, but hopefully they will be interrelated and not competitive for the talents of the people of the congregation.

Ministries that often build bridges and accelerate church growth are child care, job replacement, food distribution, drug assistance, literacy, lending libraries, and alcohol rehabilitation. Scores of other ministries exist; these are just some illustrations.

A ministering program which builds bridges to people and meets a need in the community, will provide marvelous opportunities to witness. Such ministry programs coupled with witness will result in growing churches.

Often, new converts possess talents which can be channeled into ministry programs. One young lawyer became a Christian and was speedily scheduled for an evening a week as a free legal advisor to poverty level people in a community where a new church is starting. The lawyer, because of his training, provided excellent legal advice. Because of his new birth, he was able to share his faith in Jesus Christ with those who came to see him. Doctors, dentists, teachers, counselors—all have become Christians and have donated their time to provide ministries where new churches are beginning.

Outreach

When I was a pastor, we decided to start branch Sunday Schools in three areas of our town. The church of which I was pastor was the only church of my denomination in the city, and we saw a need to establish outposts in some other sectors of the city.

It was a hard job getting the church to agree to the establishment of the branches, but after some preparation, we enlisted workers and launched our new works.

All of the Sunday Schools were held on Sunday afternoon, and the experience was tiring for most of the workers. But they continued and within a year, the combined attendance of the three branch Sunday Schools exceeded the attendance of the mother church.

The Sunday Schools were an example of outreach efforts which paid off.

The same kind of home fellowship or home Bible-study groups that were used to give birth to the mission congregations, can be used as feeders for the mission church. They can penetrate neighborhoods and continue the cultivative process of helping the new church get its roots down into the community.

Early in the life of the mission chapel, the morning programs may bo at a central place of worship, and the fellowship groups may continue as satellite units in the community. When evening worship and training activities begin at the central place, the fellowship groups might meet in the homes across the community in lieu of a midweek prayer service.

After a full church program has developed, home Bible fellowships may still be used to penetrate neighborhoods, opening homes to the witness and ministry of the church. The small groups can be an effective means for evangelistic activities.

The Sunday School can be multiplied many times over by utilizing branch Sunday Schools in the church field and adjacent areas. Branches may be in apartment complexes, community rooms, clubhouses, park shelter houses, and many other places. Church buses may be used to increase attendance. Such branches may either be at different times from the church-located Sunday School or may be held simultaneously, with participants invited to go to church worship services if they desire. The branches also can be held on a different day and become Monday Schools or Thursday Schools. There are many ways for the creative mission pastor to use branch Sunday Schools in outreach activities.

Backyard Bible Clubs are a tremendous outreach tool, and any church can have multiple Bible clubs in neighborhoods through its community. One church had thirty such clubs throughout their city one summer, followed by a Vacation Bible School at the church. The clubs served as feeders to the main church school. The church found the children, broke the ice, and enrolled many in Sunday School. Enrollment of children in Backyard Bible Clubs gives ready contact with parents, and many are thus reached for Christ.

The Educational Program

I went as a pastor to a sixty-member congregation in Eastville. The state Sunday School director offered to send one of the staffers down to help us have a Sunday School Enlargement Campaign. I didn't know for sure what one was, but I agreed to put it on.

Gladys Flowers was sent down to help us. She spotted right off that we had not made a survey, and she got up every morning at six A.M. to get the survey materials ready. Church members spent the mornings doing surveys, and we had studies on the basics of Sunday School work each night.

A few months later, we brought Gladys back to hold some age-graded workshops. She sandwiched them in everywhere; the young mothers who taught had their workshops during the mornings; other teachers came from four to six P.M.; and adult workers studied at night.

In the year that followed that initial contact, we had thirteen training courses for the teachers and officers of the educational arms of the church. The people were taught their jobs, denominational beliefs, and evangelistic techniques.

The church began to grow; departments began to bulge.

The people knew their jobs; they knew what they believed. The church grew and outreach was increased because effort was made to use the educational arm of the church to reach out to people.

The educational arms of the church include the Bible-teaching program, the training organization, missionary education, and stewardship development.

One of the foundation blocks of church planting is that the "Bible is foundational to church planting." Part of that means that the Bible is the basic tool in church-planting activities. The Sunday School is a prime growth tool for new churches. As a result, mission pastors need to enlist, train, and develop a corps of Sunday School officers and teachers. State or national Sunday School workers will be eager to help train the leadership in the Bible-teaching program.

A well-rounded program of Bible teaching and growth will include a well-planned summer Vacation Bible School along with a week of Bible study for the church. The pastor also should use regular officers' and teachers' meetings with his Sunday School workers to keep the program on course and moving ahead.

Simultaneous with the Bible-teaching program, the mission pastor also should promote and lead a training program. The first convert needs new-member training. Initial training may consist of one-to-one counseling, guidance in reading and discussion. After the mission begins to grow, a training leader needs to be designated and equipped. As the nucleus grows, a small fellowship group studying doctrine and church membership may be advisable. When the group grows sufficiently, age-grading is imperative to solidify the group, to develop and equip them to serve effectively. Again, a state, regional, or national church-training department can provide materials, counsel, and guidance on developing a training program.

The new congregation also needs to have missionary education. Such education increases the vision of the church to encompass the entire world. From the beginning, missionary education should be before the church. As soon as strength allows, a missionary education leader should be designated to be the contact person with the national missionary education offices, to receive materials and to keep the information before the church.

When the church develops sufficiently, missionary education organizations for men, women, youth, and children should be established. Regional or national missionary educational organizations will be helpful in assisting with the organization of these units.

The mission pastor also should give early attention to stewardship development or stewardship education. He should not be afraid to mention stewardship, tithing, giving, or money. He should approach the subject boldly but lovingly. Stewardship can be communicated in sermons, in lay testimonies, in special Sunday School lessons, in brochures, in films, and in other special materials.

Special programs are available from the regional or national stewardship offices and can be obtained in varying degrees of intensity. They range from soft-sell materials to full-blown stewardship campaigns which range over several weeks. The mission congregation normally would use the simple one-week plans until the congregation has sufficient numbers of people to staff the larger emphases.

Music

Much already has been written in this chapter about music and the pastor. A further word is needed to emphasize the necessity for being flexible in music style. A working-class congregation normally will prefer simple gospel songs, the middle-class church will welcome a mix of hymns and gospel songs, and the upper class with more training in music appreciation generally desire more stately hymns and anthems. To grow a mission church, music needs to fit the cultural tastes of the community which is being penetrated.

Appendix A

COMMUNITY PROFILE

DEPARTMENT OF CHURCH EXTENSION
HOME MISSION BOARD, SOUTHERN BAPTIST CONVENTION

Name of Area/Community:_____ State:_____

<u>SECTION I - THE COMMUNITY</u>:

1. Population: Now_____ 1970_____ 1960_____

2. Dimensions (approximate miles): North-South_____ East-West_____

3. Type of Housing (percent): Single Family____% Low-Rise Apartments____%

   Town House____% High-Rise Apartments____%

4. Age of Housing: When was most of the housing built?_____
   Years

5. Type of Community: Inner City ☐   Established Neighborhood ☐

   Suburban ☐ Exurban ☐ Small Town ☐ Open Country ☐

<u>SECTION II - THE PEOPLE</u>:

6. Age Characteristics (percent): Under 18 Years____% 18-39 Years_____%

   40-64 Years_____% 65 Years or More____%

7. Race (percent): White_____% Negro_____% Other_____ _____%
   Name

8. Family Structure: Young Families With Children ☐   Young Couples ☐

   Older Families Without Children ☐   Singles ☐

9. Employment: White Collar ☐   Blue Collar ☐   Military ☐

   University ☐   Other_____ ☐

10. Family Income Groups (percent): Less Than $4,000____% $4,000-$7,999____%

    $8,000-$11,999____% $12,000-$15,999____%

    $16,000-$19,000____% $20,000 or More____%

11. Nativity (percent): This State_____% This Region_____% Abroad_____%

12. Educational Attainment (percent): Grammar School____% High School_____%

    College_____%

SECTION III - THE CHURCHES

13. On the chart below, please rank in descending order by size of total member-
    ship these denominations in the first column: Baptist, Catholic, Methodist,
    Presbyterian, Congregational, Christian, Episcopal, Lutheran, Pentacostal
    (all kinds), Jewish, and others. Then complete the information requested
    on each denomination.

LIST OF DENOMINATIONS	NUMBER		
	CHURCHES	MEMBERS	AVER. ATTEND.

Appendix B

AREA ANALYSIS FOR CHURCH EXTENSION

This analysis should be made before plans are finalized for the new church extension.

_____   _____   _____
(city)   (county)   (state)

Area's name (description of geographical area) _____

Association _____

1. RELIGIOUS DATA (Resource: personal interviews, telephone yellow pages, and observation):

   (1) How many denominations are presently represented in this area?

	Churches	Members
Southern Baptist	_____	_____
Other Baptist	_____	_____
Other evangelical	_____	_____
Catholic	_____	_____
Other nonevangelical	_____	_____
Jewish	_____	_____
Other religions	_____	_____
TOTAL	_____	_____

   (2) Rank the denominations represented in the area by name and membership:

Rank denominations by membership and write in names.	Number members	Number attendants	Number churches
1			
2			
3			
4			
5			

   (3) What percent of the people in the area attend religious services?

   Weekly_____ Monthly_____ Seldom_____ Never_____ = 100%

(4) Does any Southern Baptist church attempt to reach this area now? _____

How? _____

_____

(5) Name the nearest Southern Baptist church. _____

    a. How many miles is it from this area? _____

    b. What economic groups does it reach best?_____

(6) Name the Southern Baptist church(es) that is the logical one to sponsor this new work. _____

_____

(7) How many unchurched persons are there in this area?

Unchurched persons	Number	Percent*
Baptist preference?		
Other preference?		
TOTAL		100%
Names and addresses in hand		
Have expressed an interest		

2. POPULATION DATA (Resource: 1970 Census and Planning Commission):

    (1) What is the present population of the area by the racial and age groups listed below?

Racial Groups

Types	Number	Percent*
White		
Negro		
Spanish surname		
Other_____		
TOTAL		100%

Age Groups

By years	Number	Percent*
0-17 years		
18-34 years		
35-64 years		
65 and over		
TOTAL		100%

*Percent is calculated by dividing the total into the number in each group.

(2) What are the present housing trends in this area?

Occupancy	Number	Percent*		Type Housing	Units	Percent*
Owner				Single family		
Renter				Multifamily		
				Mobile home		
TOTAL		100%		TOTAL		100%

*Percent is calculated by dividing the total into the number in each group.

(3) Is this area's population (check more than one):   Stable ☐   Growing ☐   New ☐

Declining ☐   Proposed ☐   Other ☐ _____

3. ECONOMIC DATA (Resource: Local office employment agency for State and Planning Commission)

(1) Describe the economy of the area. (agriculture, manufacturing, mining, government installations and insti-

tutions, military, commerce and trade, tourism, recreation, other) _____

(2) What are the five largest job classifications represented in the area? (agriculture, manufacturing, construc-

tion, transportation, trade, finance, service, mining and government) _____

_____

(3) What percentage of the people are in each of the two following categories?

Employment Groups	Percent		Income Groups	Percent
Professional			Less than $3,000	
Office workers			$3,000 - $4,999	
Skilled			$5,000 $6,999	
Semiskilled			$7,000 - $9,999	
Unskilled			$10,000 - $14,999	
			$15,000 and over	
TOTAL	100%		TOTAL	100%

4. INSTITUTIONAL DATA (school board, planning commission and observation):

(1) What educational institutions are present in the area?

Institution	Schools	Students
Primary		
Secondary		
Technical		
College and university		
TOTAL		

(2) Name any public institutions in the area. (mental or VA hospitals, prison, military, etc.) _____

_____

(3) Name any private institutions in the area. (retirement centers, rest homes, nursing homes, etc.) _____

_____

5. SUMMARY:

Use a separate sheet to write a summary of the area as you see it, and give your suggestions as to how this new work should begin (fellowship Bible class, VBS, branch Sunday School, chapel, revival, community ministries, week-day ministry, others).

This analysis was made by _____ Date_____

Position_____ of Association_____ State _____

Evaluated by _____ Evaluated by . _____
          (associational superintendent of missions)   (state missions director)

If church pastoral aid is involved, make six copies of this survey—one each for: superintendent of missions; moderator; chairman of missions committee; sponsoring church; director of missions; Department of Church Extension, Home Mission Board, 1350 Spring Street, NW, Atlanta, Georgia 30309, (404) 873-4041.

NOTE—A copy of this survey must precede or accompany each application for church pastoral aid.

Appendix C

SCORE SHEET FOR NEW WORK PRIORITY

List communities and rate from 1-10.

See pages ___ for priorities questions.	Buckhead	Palmetto	Sandy Springs	Decatur														
Population?	4	6	9	10														
Churched?	3	4	7	7														
Response?	3	3	5	6														
Potential?	4	5	7	9														
Strategic?	3	4	7	7														
Influence?	4	5	6	8														
Self-Support?	4	5	8	8														
Resources?	3	5	8	8														
Sponsorship?	4	5	7	9														
Field?	3	4	6	8														
Nucleus?	4	5	7	7														
Personnel?	3	4	5	7														
Alternative?	4	5	6	8														
Total?	46	60	87	103														
Score Number	4	3	2	1														
Rating	L	M	H	VH														

1. Select communities from compilation.
2. Rate 1-10.   1-lowest rating;   10-highest rating.
   Rating is relative and communities must be compared to each other in each area.
3. Score: highest #1, next highest #2, etc.
4. Rating is a relative guide to help determine priorities:
   20-50 low, 50-75 medium, 75-100 high, 100-130 very high

Appendix D

AREA RELIGIOUS SURVEY

1. ASSIGNMENT DESIGNATION		2. IF INCOMPLETE, WHY? ☐ ☐ ☐ NOT HOME ☐ REFUSED

3. FAMILY NAME *Last Name Only*	4. ADDRESS

5. TELEPHONE NUMBER	6. COMMENTS: *If necessary*

PLEASE FILL IN THESE COLUMNS FOR EACH NAME LISTED

10. OMIT *For Processing Only*	11. FIRST NAME or initials of each person in this family at this address *(Separate card for separate families)*	CHURCH MEMBER		14. NAME OF LOCAL CHURCH If column 12 is YES And 13 is *YES* — Enter local church membership. And 13 is *NO* — Enter local church preference — if none, enter denominational membership. If column 12 is *NO* Enter local church or denominational preference — if no preference, enter "none".	15. Attend Church Monthly Y - yes N - no	16. Attend Sunday School Y - yes N - no	17. Year of Birth
		12. ANY-WHERE Y - yes N - no	13. LOCAL Y - yes N - no				

20. THIS INFORMATION IS RESTRICTED TO CHURCH USE ONLY

Appendix E

The following is the front page of a four-page pamphlet for each telephone canvasser. These are available from the Missouri Baptist Press.

INSTRUCTION FOR THE TELEPHONE CANVASSER

(Survey to Find Unchurched Families)

A. GENERAL NOTES

1. This survey is to locate unchurched people.
2. It is important that you be familiar with the proper procedures to be followed in this survey. Study these instructions very carefully.
3. Telephone every family in your assignment packet. Do not call the business or commercial places.
4. Do not fill out a card on churched families. Fill out a card only on families with unchurched persons. This will enable you to call more families in the same amount of time.
5. Your attitude and approach in this survey is of tremendous importance.
6. If anyone asks you why you are doing this, explain that it is to help the church better minister to the community.

B. DO MOST OF YOUR CANVASSING ON SATURDAY

1. Saturday is the best day for canvassing. Do all the canvassing you can on Saturday.
2. In case you do not finish on Saturday then finish on Sunday. Try to have at least 90% of your calling completed by Sunday night.
3. Use Monday to canvass those not home over the week-end.

C. THE GENERAL PROCEDURE

1. Please be accurate. Get the correct information. Get all the information requested. Write so others can read it.
2. Let the telephone ring four or five times and if no one answers then hang up. Put "NA" by the family where there is no answer.
3. If the telephone is busy then put "B" by that family.
4. Go through the entire assignment and then try those where there was no answer on the first call. On all call backs let the telephone ring six or seven times.
5. If a person refuses to give the information (and only a few will refuse) then put "R" by that family. Be kind and courteous in all cases. Do not argue. Get what information a person will give you and thank him.
6. If the telephone has been disconnected then put "D" by that family.
7. If a different family has the telephone other than the family listed on the assignment then get all the normal information on that family.
8. Write with pencil. It is easier to correct a mistake.
9. Fill out a card on the unchurched families only. Do not fill out any card on the churched families. You are to determine in the opening part of the interview whether the family is churched or unchurched. If you determine that the family is unchurched then fill out a card on that family.
10. An unchurched family is a family with one or more persons age 17 or older who does not attend at least monthly.
11. If every person in the family age 17 or older attends at least monthly—then do not fill out a card on that family.
12. If there is anyone in the family age 17 or older who does not attend at least monthly—then fill out a card on that entire family.

D. BEFORE YOU DIAL

1. If the family name is not familiar and easy to pronounce then pronounce it out loud a few times to familiarize yourself with the pronounciation. It is important to try to pronounce the name properly in the interview. Remember that it may have been mispronounced before.
2. Have a pencil and note paper ready for making notes during the interview.
3. Be familiar with all the questions on the survey card.
4. Review these Instructions for the Telephone Canvasser

S–76–A

An attractive feature of this plan is the expandable auditorium. When the church grows to need more space, the temporary walls in the Preschool, Children, and Youth rooms can be removed to increase the auditorium seating capacity to 195 (pews - 180, choir - 15). Twenty more seating can be added by replacing the preschool B–3 wall with a folding door. The departments and classrooms lost can be included in the next building which would be an educational unit.

The plan may be the first of a two unit plan, or the first unit of a master plan with several units. If planned to be the permanent auditorium of a two unit plan, it should have a high ceiling using scissors trusses, or laminated wood beams.

The Preschool and Children's departments provide twenty square feet per person. The total building has 2,282 square feet of floor space.

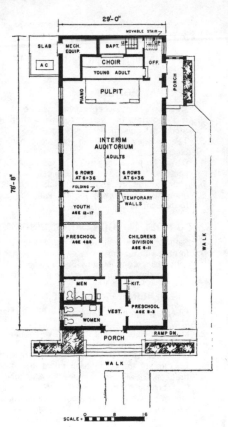

INTERIM AUDITORIUM SCHEDULE

PEWS	72
CHOIR	15
TOTAL PERMANENT SEATS	87
CLASSROOM	13
GROSS TOTAL	100

EDUCATIONAL PROGRAM SCHEDULE

	AGES	NUMBER OF DEPARTMENTS	TOTAL CLASSES	ATTENDANCE CAPACITY
PRESCHOOL	B–3	1		5
	4–5	1		6
CHILDREN	6–11	1		11
YOUTH	12–17	1	1	9
ADULT	18 up	1	2	30
TOTAL				61

Appendix G

M–152–C

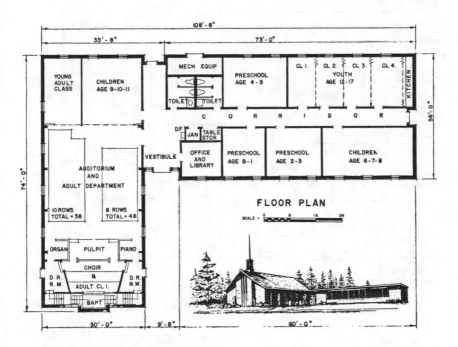

FLOOR PLAN

SCALE = 0   8   16   24

INTERIM AUDITORIUM SCHEDULE

PEWS	108
CHOIR	26
TOTAL	134

EDUCATIONAL PROGRAM SCHEDULE

	AGES	NUMBER OF DEPART-MENTS	TOTAL CLASSES	ATTEN-DANCE CAPACITY
PRESCHOOL	B–3	2		11
	4–5	1		10
CHILDREN	6–11	2		24
YOUTH	12–17	1	3	27
ADULT	18–29	1	1	10
	30 up	1	3	48
TOTAL				130

This attractive unit is designed to satisfy a church's aesthetic desire for the first unit to look like a completed church building. The auditorium may easily become the chapel in the master plan, or it can be converted to a fellowship area, or used for educational purposes. There is good access to the building from the rear and one end of the educational wing, as well as the main front entrance. The auditorium vestibule serves as the traffic connection with the educational portion of the building.

Preschool and Children's departments have twenty-five square feet per person. The building has 4,440 square feet of floor space.

Appendix H

S–118

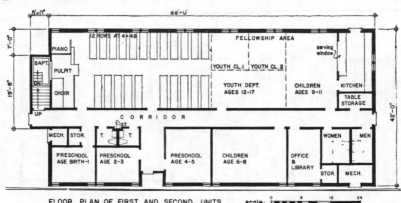

FLOOR PLAN OF FIRST AND SECOND UNITS   scale:
S-118

INTERIM AUDITORIUM SCHEDULE

PEWS	98
CHOIR	8
TOTAL PERMANENT SEATS	106
CLASSROOMS	40
GROSS TOTAL	146

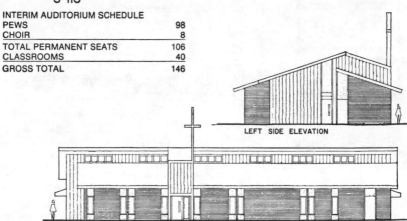

LEFT SIDE ELEVATION

FRONT ELEVATION

EDUCATIONAL PROGRAM SCHEDULE

	AGES	NUMBER OF DEPART-MENTS	TOTAL CLASSES	ATTEN-DANCE CAPACITY
PRESCHOOL	B–5	3		18
CHILDREN	6–11	2		28
YOUTH	12–17	1	2	24
ADULT	18 up	1	3	48
TOTAL				118

This plan may be used as a first unit, or as the second stage arrangement of plan S–68. 1,946 square feet are added to S–68 for a total of 3,794 square feet.

Space for preschoolers and children is provided at twenty square feet per person.